LABRADOR VILLAGE

LABRADOR VILLAGE

John C. Kennedy

Memorial University of Newfoundland

WAVELAND

PRESS, INC.

Prospect Heights, Illinois

For information about this book, write or call:
    Waveland Press, Inc.
    P.O. Box 400
    Prospect Heights, Illinois 60070
    (708) 634-0081

Cover photographs: Lodge Bay children play on a boat slipway (top); the oldest and largest house in Cape Charles, where the author lived in 1979 and 1980 (bottom). Water photograph: Phil Brodatz.

Copyright © 1996 by Waveland Press, Inc.

ISBN 0-88133-863-X

Printed in the United States of America

7   6   5   4   3   2   1

Contents

Preface

Many of the small fishing settlements dotting Canada's east coast are presently struggling to survive. During recent decades, and increasingly of late, the size and numbers of several vital species—particularly codfish—have steadily declined. Since 1992, cod has vanished altogether in some places, leaving nearby communities wholly dependent on Canadian government support. Just what caused this dramatic decline of cod and other species continues to be debated, though all agree that the fishery crisis is both an ecological and a social disaster. Many people inside and outside the fishery believe that many communities may die, much as when midwest prairie farmers abandoned their farms during the Dust Bowl era of the 1930s. What were these fishing settlements like during the years prior to the present crisis?

Although this book begins and ends with that crisis, the research started before it. After fieldwork during the early 1970s in a northern Labrador community (see Kennedy 1982), I began teaching anthropology at Memorial University of Newfoundland in St. John's, Newfoundland, Canada's most recently formed province. In the mid-1970s, I launched a new course specifically on Labrador peoples (Labrador Society and Culture) but was repeatedly frustrated by the lack of information on communities along Labrador's southeastern coast. By the late 1970s I decided to take matters in hand and head to the southeastern coast. I conducted fieldwork in the winter settlement of Lodge Bay, living with one family between February and early June 1979 and then accompanying another family to the summer fishing station at Cape Charles, where I lived until August. Consequently, I lived with two very different families in the two seasonal settlements used by Lodge Bay–Cape Charles folk. I supplemented the brief 1979 research period with short visits to Cape Charles during the summer of 1980 and the spring of 1992. I also spent three months in each of two other southeastern Labrador communities—Port Hope Simpson in 1982 and Cartwright in 1983. This fieldwork stimulated further archival research, resulting in a baseline anthropological history of the southeastern Labrador region (Kennedy 1995).

Field anthropology creates an intense, personal alliance between the anthropologist as stranger, and the local people. In sharing the daily activities of household and community, anthropologists become privileged outsiders, learning many secrets they can never reveal. This creates certain ethical dilemmas in describing the way of life witnessed and, to a degree, participated in. What issues are locally considered to be sensitive? Should the real names of people or communities be used and if so, how can people be protected? I have tried to resolve these and other similar dilemmas as I believe Lodge Bay people would wish: I have not disguised the name of their community; I have used pseudonyms for all persons living during the 1979 field period; and I have not listed the names of the people whom I quote from the field.

I thank Memorial University's Institute of Social and Economic Research for funding the 1979, 1980, and 1992 field research in Lodge Bay and Cape Charles. I also thank Mark Dolomount, Leslie Tuff, and Greg White, who helped on the manuscript over the past three summers, as Challenge (SEED) grant students. Thanks are also due to Dan Bergeron, who read an earlier version of the book and made many excellent suggestions. I also thank Mark Tate, Louis Chiaramonte, and John Doyle for their comments on chapter 1, and Peter Narváez, and Herbert and Violetta Halpert for their comments on some of the folk narratives presented in chapter 5.

Thanks also go to Wayne, Dora, and Billy Rumbolt for their hospitality during my occasional visits to Mary's Harbour and to the Reverend Donald and Shirley Fowler, then serving in Mary's Harbour.

I acknowledge the loving support of my wife, Karen Olsson. Karen is a former Grenfell mission Labrador nurse with considerable knowledge of and affection for Labrador people. She granted me the time away from household responsibilities necessary to write; commented on earlier drafts; and was indispensable during the final rewrite, here in northern Norway, where I am conducting new research. And to our young sons, Alexander and Erik, a simple thanks.

Finally, my sincere appreciation goes to the people of Lodge Bay; this is their book. I dedicate the book to the whole community, and I especially thank Margaret and Clifford Pye and Aunt Violet and (the late) Uncle Frank Pye.

John C. Kennedy
Årviksand, Norway

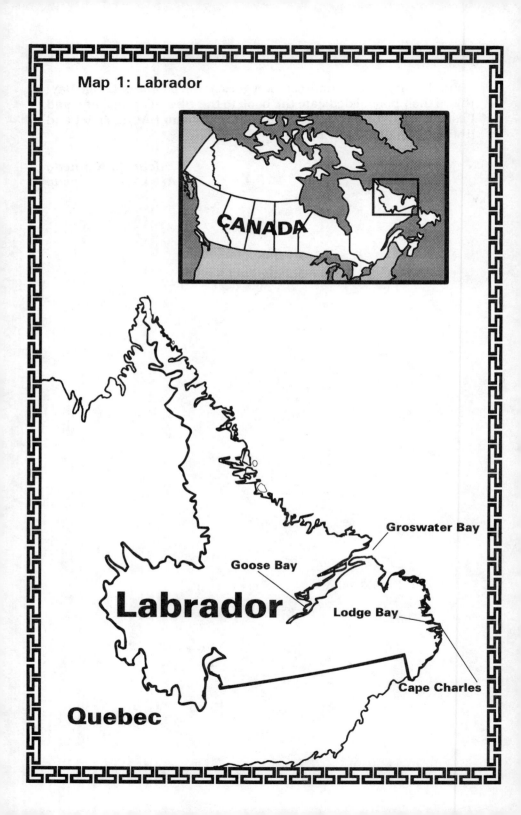

Map 1: Labrador

CANADA

Groswater Bay

Goose Bay

Labrador

Lodge Bay

Cape Charles

Quebec

Chapter 1

Introduction

Gray clouds hugged the rocky headlands of Cape Charles, on the southeastern coast of Labrador. My routine on this cold morning in late June began as usual. I walked toward the end of a wooden fishing stage attached to the land immediately in front of the 100-year-old house where I boarded. The *stage* was a log scaffolding perched over the icy waters of Injun Cove. It supported *flakes* where fishers once air-dried salted codfish; the stage also supported a large, two-story storehouse and smaller *fish store* where salted codfish were temporarily piled in layered *bulks*. My immediate destination was an old outhouse poised over the water at the end of the stage. My aim was to relieve myself; Cape Charles lacked indoor toilets, community-wide electricity, and other modern conveniences.

Hearing the rhythmic put-put-put of a *motorboat* engine, I walked over to the fish store, where Jim and his fishing crew had just returned from checking their *cod traps*. Jim, his younger brother Tom, and Sid, Jim's son, all wore standard fishing attire: heavy flannel shirts, black rubber *oilskins* over their green work pants, and high rubber boots with tops turned down.

Other than such facts as these, outward appearances often deceive. Like many of his peers, Jim appeared a rough man, the threatening kind one avoided in a crowd. His leathery skin and wrinkled face made him appear older than his forty years. Yet Jim's

Note: Regarding the use of italics in this book, readers should note that, upon first instance, local terms and expressions are italicized in order to indicate that a full definition of the word or phrase can be found in Appendix 1.

1

Boats, fishing stage and fish stores at Cape Charles, 1980.

rugged demeanor stemmed from his life on the Labrador land and sea—a life of hunting, trapping, and fishing. His coarse appearance masked a warm and generous personality.

"Any fish?" I asked. "Naw, pretty scarce," Jim answered. "We might have a *quintal* (112 pounds) or so." Tom secured the boat, and then he and Sid began forking the codfish from the *cuddy* (enclosure) of their nine-meter (thirty-foot) open motorboat onto the deck of the stage. Meanwhile, several of Tom's and Jim's children appeared out of nowhere to watch and learn about that morning's catch, then disappeared with news soon current throughout the tiny fishing settlement. Before leaving Jim's crew to the task of splitting open and salting their meager catch, I asked whether they had heard how other crews had done that morning. "I don' know," he said. "We saw Don and them but don' know how they got on."

I returned to the house where I boarded, that of *Uncle* Paul and *Aunt* Susan, who were Jim and Tom's parents, and the oldest people in Cape Charles. Aunt Susan browned my *toast bread* at the wood-burning range while Uncle Paul sat with one leg up on the *daybed* beneath the kitchen window, drawing on his pipe. "Any fish?" he asked as I entered. My answer did not surprise him, and he predicted, "And there'll be nothing until this eastern wind clears out." Later, I would record Uncle Paul's association between wind and fish; it would join other threads in this account of the fabric of local life. Another day of anthropological fieldwork had begun.

My time with the people of Cape Charles began at Lodge Bay, where they wintered. It's there, really, where this book begins. In 1979, the ethnographic present of this book, 125 people lived at Lodge Bay where they hunted, harvested wood, built boats, and depended on various sources of cash. Each summer most of these same people moved their families and some household belongings by boat to the barren Labrador coast, mainly to Cape Charles, to fish for salmon, codfish, herring, and other marine species.

Lodge Bay is roughly nineteen kilometers (twelve miles) west of Cape Charles. In fact, the two villages form one community; they are seasonal villages largely occupied by the same people. The summer fishing station of Cape Charles collectively refers to two settlements, Injun Cove and nearby Wall's Tickle (locally called the Cove and the Tickle). The wooden houses at Cape Charles are heated by wood stoves, some have gravity-fed cold water plumbing, connected each summer, and all have diesel generators that provide a few hours of electricity each day. In 1979, a seasonal school operated at the Cove, near the small church and herring plant. Two of the three merchants with stores in Lodge Bay have smaller, seasonal operations at Cape Charles.

The houses of the winter settlement of Lodge Bay nestle along both sides of the St. Charles River. They tend to be larger than those at the Cape and, in 1979, some had interior plumbing; all were served by community-wide electricity generated at Mary's Harbour. The school (which doubles as a church), community hall, post office, and one small retail store is on the south side, while two other retail stores are on the north side.

Lodge Bay is some 550 kilometers (340 miles) northwest of St. John's, the capital city of the Canadian province of Newfoundland and about twice that distance northeast of Montreal, Quebec (see map 1). Even in the 1990s, Lodge Bay, like other communities in southeastern Labrador, is relatively remote. It is accessible year-round by small plane and in summer by boat. The only road out of the community, built in the early 1980s, is the ten-kilometer gravel road meandering north through the sheltered forests and rocky uplands to the larger center of Mary's Harbour, its 1991 population 470.

Lodge Bay is one of eleven winter communities in southeastern Labrador. The people wintering in these eleven communities have always dispersed each summer to coastal fishing settlements. In 1991, the combined population of the region's eleven winter

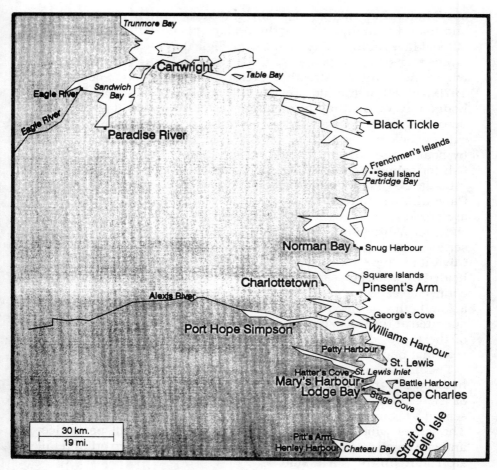

Map 2: Southeastern Labrador

communities was 2,962, that of many small North American towns. All are tiny communities. Norman Bay is the smallest, with a population of 58 in 1991. That same year, Cartwright, the largest, had a population of 611.

It may be difficult to imagine living your life in a rural village of a few hundred people, a place where you know more than you might wish about every single person. Many of us come from large cities where we are accustomed to the daily anonymity of shopping malls or city streets. Small communities can be very intimate places where, as Berger (1979, 10) astutely observes, "the difference between what is known about a person and what is unknown is slight."

While the small-scale communities of the world are always changing, distinctive in language and custom, they share certain structural similarities. That is, the structure of social relationships in the small villages of Spain, Malaysia, or Ireland is often surprisingly similar. Sociologists and social anthropologists have produced a rich literature describing and analyzing small communities. One brief example from this literature, drawn from so-called typological tradition, provides a useful comparative window through which to begin to understand Lodge Bay society.

For me, the social anthropology of small communities begins with sociologist Ferdinand Tönnies's 1887 classic *Gemeinschaft und Gesellschaft*. Like others writing in the typological tradition (including Emile Durkheim, Max Weber, Robert Redfield, Talcott Parsons, and others), Tönnies contrasts two types of societies, according to the characteristic kinds of social interaction or association usually found in them. The social life of *Gemeinschaft*, or community (think here of the smallest you know), is intimate, creative, communal, and sacred; whereas that of *Gesellschaft*, or society (or association—think here of any city), is distant, repetitive, contractual, and profane. As with some of the other nineteenth- and early twentieth-century typological theories, there was in the 1887 classic an element of pastoral romanticism, lamenting the wane of rurality and resulting disappearance of the Gemeinschaft into which Tönnies was born. The heart of Tönnies's dichotomy is his contrast between the natural will of the countryside and the rational will of the city. Natural will summarizes the common goods, sentiments, and fates shared by rural folk, and for the peasant, these alone are ends in themselves. In Gemeinschafts like Lodge Bay, all are in it together, and the *it* is everything of experience, importance, and meaning. One way of illustrating Tönnies's concept of natural will is to think of someone you have always been especially fond of but have not seen in a long time, perhaps a cherished but distant grandfather or aunt. Now imagine that right now you could be with that person. How would you feel? Very likely, just being with them would fill you with sensations of emotional warmth and ease; togetherness would be a mutually satisfying goal in itself, and little else would be necessary. The natural will characteristic of Gemeinschaft applies to whole communities built on such togetherness, communities in which most social relationships contain this interdependent sense of warmth, fellowship, and intimacy. These tend to be small human communities, where people share so much that just being together is sufficient. Lodge Bay is such a place, even though contemporary residents, perhaps like all those living in changing Gemeinschafts, claim that it was once even more so. Lodge Bay people today complain that people are not so close now, compared with *them times*, a time when people were more dependent on each other. Such a complaint is, like the essence of Tönnies's dichotomy, about the decline of Gemeinschaft.

There are many definitions of community (Hillary 1955; Kaufman 1959; Lyon 1987; and Cohen 1985), leading L. Lyon to complain that in the social sciences "there seems to be an inverse relationship between the importance of a concept and the precision with which it is defined" (1987, 4). Here, I use a structural meaning of community, that is, as a social and cultural collectivity of people adapted to a locally defined geographic space.

Community studies have long been a method and object of empirical research by geographers, sociologists, and anthropologists (see Arensberg and Kimbell 1965; Bell and Newby 1978; Clark 1973). The many community studies discussed in these overviews examine far too many foci to summarize here, but let me mention one: the relationship between changing patterns of economy and inheritance, social atrophy, and mental health, as presented in several Irish community studies (Arensberg [1937]; Scheper-Hughes [1979]; and Brody [1982]). What's more, the pathetic Ballybran bachelors Nancy Scheper-Hughes so poignantly describes have their counterparts in Lodge Bay, as do (albeit in a different context) the Spanish bachelors (*mozos*) described by Ruth Behar (1991). In short, some understanding of the sociology of small communities is of use in approaching Lodge Bay.

This book is a community study, based largely on ethnographic methods. Ethnography is the branch of sociocultural anthropology that describes the customs of peoples around the world. I sketch the minutiae of daily life in this subarctic community, accompanying fishers to their fishing grounds in summer and into the Labrador forests in winter to hunt, to trap, and to cut wood. We also learn about Labrador family life, about the ways in which children are raised, about patterned social interaction, and about local belief systems. My aim is mainly descriptive. Although the period described is 1979, some characteristics of local life continue, while others are threatened by change.

Culture

I use the term culture in its expressive and symbolic sense, to refer to a learned, shared, and relatively integrated symbol system that includes the kinds of knowledge necessary for practical existence and the values or goals of a particular human group. Necessarily, culture is an abstraction, and many ethnographic case studies sometimes fail to define such important terms. My sense of the term begins with the observation that anthropologists generally study groups of people rather than individuals. The anthropological language for such groups includes terms such as culture, society, community, and so on. However, anthropologists do not exclusively own these important terms. Biological scientists, for example, describe communities of microorganisms or bacteria as cultures, and this important anthropological term is also widely used to refer to artistic endeavors or, as an adjective, to characterize the refined sensitivity necessary to appreciate civilized accomplishments. Since the late nineteenth century, however, anthropology has urged another meaning of culture to be a shared way of life learned by a human group, including the rules and assumptions underlying patterned social action.

The culture of Lodge Bay people springs from European and aboriginal sources. Henceforth, I use the term Settler (capitalized for a people) to refer to the earliest Europeans to permanently settle in Labrador, and their English-speaking descendants. The earliest English emigrants arriving in southeastern Labrador in the nineteenth century brought with them their West Country English dialect and ideas about the meaning of work and play, time and space, life and death, and good and evil. However, since the Settlers established settlements in southeastern Labrador, their lives have been continuously influenced by generations of Newfoundland fishers who visited the Labrador coast each summer to fish. The annual contact between Labrador Settlers and transient Newfoundlanders makes it difficult to distinguish which elements of Settler culture may be traced directly to West England and which were developed in Newfoundland.

Like peoples everywhere, Lodge Bay folk assign their own meanings to the colors, sights, sounds, and shapes that surround them. Let us take, for example, the color green, the color of the spruce and balsam fir trees that encircle Lodge Bay homes. Green has several local cultural associations, one of them touching on religion. While Lodge Bay is too small to justify a resident Anglican (Church of England) minister, people take their formal religion seriously, maintaining a church at Cape Charles for occasional use by the visiting minister from Mary's Harbour. The color green, one man somewhat facetiously remarked as we stood admiring the freshly painted dark green trim on his neighbor's fish storehouse at Cape Charles, is "no good because it's too Irish," meaning too

Catholic. (The ethnographer's task is to piece together such utterances, cautiously discarding those considered idiosyncratic, and to seek associations among them in an effort to understand the workings and meanings of local culture.)

The second major root of Settler culture is Inuit (Eskimo), who once inhabited southeastern Labrador. It is important to add that all contemporary Labrador Inuit live along Labrador's northern coast. Some of the historic technology used by Lodge Bay people derives from ancient Inuit practices, although older people know little about historic or contemporary Labrador Inuit or about the origins of such technologies. For example, during the now-fabled dog team era, which ended in the 1960s, Lodge Bay and other southeastern Labrador men used corruptions of Inuktitut (Inuit language) words for commanding dog teams to veer right (*uuk*) or left (*utta*); sled dogs pulled long wooden sleds, called by their Inuit name, *komatiks*; Settlers also used the Inuit knife, the curvilinear *ulu*, to scrape fat from the interior of sealskins without perforating the skin. Settlers used such technologies tacitly, knowing little about the origins or the original meaning Inuit had attached to such practices. During the 1980s, however, the development of a new aboriginal (native or indigenous) political organization (the Labrador Metis Association) has caused Settlers—both those with and without Inuit blood—to reconsider customs of Inuit origin that were previously practiced without thought (Kennedy 1988). Ever-changing social or political circumstances can encourage a people to reevaluate the meaning of cultural practices and to attach new and explicit meaning to their use.

Fieldwork

Fieldwork is the anthropological method whereby the anthropologist (or ethnographer) lives in a community, observing and recording all characteristics of daily life. Anthropological convention recommends informing the community about the proposed research, and I attempted to do this in the Lodge Bay case.

My reason for wanting to conduct fieldwork in southeastern Labrador was that very little was known about communities in the region. Indeed, prior to my research there, I was not sure how many of the communities shown on maps still existed, since a government relocation scheme in the 1960s and 1970s had closed many. Before deciding on Lodge Bay, I communicated with several individuals and groups in Labrador knowledgeable about southeastern Labrador. I wanted to select an appropriate community and to inform the community of my research intentions. I first contacted a regional pan-Labrador organization, the Labrador Resources Advisory Council (LRAC), seeking their suggestions for an appropriate community. I sought similar advice from persons working for the Memorial University Extension Service and *Them Days* magazine. This led me to choose Lodge Bay and its summer fishing settlement at Cape Charles. These contacts introduced me to a Lodge Bay man living in Goose Bay, Labrador, whom I interviewed, and the LRAC arranged for me to board with a family in Lodge Bay. I departed for Lodge Bay erroneously assuming people there knew (and presumably approved of) my plans.

The early part of winter 1979 was unusually mild. Fog, wet snow, and generally unsettled weather enshrouded much of Newfoundland and Labrador. Consequently, I was delayed almost one week in St. John's awaiting the one-and-a-half-hour jet flight northwest to Goose Bay, where I then spent another week awaiting a flight south to Lodge Bay.

I was the only passenger bound for Lodge Bay on the Labrador Airways flight south. The trip first took us over frozen Lake Melville, the 200-kilometer-long estuary cutting from the coast into the Labrador interior. We passed over the low, undulating Mealy Mountains, over valleys bordering frozen rivers, and over exposed patches of tundra ringed by dark boreal forest. After brief stops in the Sandwich Bay communities of Paradise River and Cartwright, the old De Havilland Otter airplane droned its way south, following the seacoast. From my window on the left of the plane the Labrador coast appeared a vivid contrast of whites and blue grays. The snow-covered sea ice covered all bays and extended out over the ocean several kilometers from the easternmost capes and headlands. Open ocean was sometimes visible beyond the edge of the sea ice. The monotony of the sea ice was also occasionally broken by patches of open water, particularly at *tickles* between islands, where ocean currents prevented the sea from freezing.

The mesmerizing overload of this frozen vista eventually closed my eyelids, but I jolted to attention as we began our descent into Charlottetown. Our stay there was brief, and the skiplane soon bounced its way down the frozen lake runway, rose above the trees, and headed south again, for Williams Harbour and Lodge Bay. The plane landed on the frozen St. Charles River, which separates the north and south sides of this riverine community, downriver and out of sight of any houses. The trip from Goose Bay had taken two and a quarter hours. No one came to meet the plane. As the plane taxied away, its propellers wafted puffs of snow at me. Like other anthropologists at similarly lonely times, I momentarily wondered about my decision to leave the comfort of my university post for what seemed an uncertain future.

My musings were soon interrupted by the buzz of a snowmobile (locally called a *skidoo*) rounding a point of land and heading over the snow-covered ice in my direction. The young driver stopped beside me, my suitcase, and duffel bag. Uneasily communicating as much by gesture as by word, the young man assured me that his snowmobile could carry the two of us, plus my baggage, and motioned that I climb aboard. I did so. He stood on the running board up front, and I sat behind, holding my baggage. Minutes later we stopped by the door of a small, two-story wooden house. My driver helped carry my bags into the enclosed porch and then shyly accompanied me into the kitchen, perchance to witness my introduction and thus learn who I was. Within, I met my hosts, a young couple, with four children between the ages of three and nine years. After introductions, I was shown to my room, a tiny cubicle furnished with a single bed and dresser. A plastic pail, my toilet, sat in a corner by the door. It was with some guilt that I later learned that my room belonged to two of my host's children and that they had been moved in with their siblings to make room for me!

Over the next few days, I learned that my hosts' initial hospitality, though considerable and forever appreciated, was based on a misunderstanding. Like other villagers, my hosts understood that I worked for the University Extension Service and that my stay would be brief. My efforts (through the LRAC) to inform the community of my plans had succeeded only in increasing my anxiety about intruding into the lives of Lodge Bay people. My status became even less clear once people heard that I wanted to do research. Unlike in many areas of the Canadian north, the status of anthropologist was new to Lodge Bay people. Gradually, I became known as "the Professor" (not a nickname I would have chosen): an inquisitive, curious stranger who would instantly pull a small black notebook from his shirt pocket to record locally obvious facts of everyday life.

I would later learn that my host's house was representative of many southeastern Labrador homes. The first floor consisted of an enclosed porch entering to the kitchen and a living room. The second story consisted of three small bedrooms.

Labrador kitchens—and indeed, traditionally kitchens throughout much of Newfoundland and Labrador—are public places open to anyone in the community. Locals require no invitation to enter and sit in another's kitchen and since the custom of knocking on the door is reserved for strangers, locals often enter and sit quietly at the kitchen table or a chair by the stove. Locals may sit in

Sparkling wood range
of Lodge Bay family at
Carrol's Cove fishing
station, 1980.
(Photograph by Karen
Olsson)

another's kitchen for some time, saying little and expecting less. The Labrador visiting custom of entering another's kitchen, sitting quietly for a half hour or more and then leaving, contrasts decidedly with urban Canadian or American cultural notions about domestic space, privacy, and the meaning of silence. Insofar as sitting quietly in another's kitchen, in the company of one's comrades, is an end unto itself, this Labrador custom illustrates the "natural will" Tönnies associated with Gemeinschaft. Though conversation might occur, it is not obligatory: all share in the quiet experience of being one. In contrast, the kitchens of Vancouver or Omaha are reserved private space, the restricted domain of family members, and conversation seems necessary. If others are invited in, unspoken rules imply that it is for some purpose; it is improbable that others would simply come and sit quietly. Indeed, such an unlikely quiet gathering invokes unsettling images of concentration, distress, or

Lodge Bay couple, 1980. (Photograph by Karen Olsson)

even ignorance. Consequently, middle-class outsiders (such as nurses, teachers, or anthropologists) residing temporarily in small Labrador communities are often uncomfortable in a kitchen filled with four or five grown men sitting around saying little; outsiders need to talk and may try to relieve their unease by attempting to start a conversation.

As anthropological luck would have it, my host's kitchen served as *the* informal drop-in center for the community's unmarried young men and during such gatherings was decidedly not the typical quiet Labrador kitchen just described. Each night after supper young men gathered there to talk, play cards or darts, or simply to rendezvous before heading elsewhere. This placed me in an ideal location to hear about daily events throughout the village. That I was actually interested in such news prompted those recounting it to clarify points about which I expressed confusion. The kitchen became the classroom for my accelerated course on the community. My initial teachers—my hosts and their nightly visitors—patiently tolerated my intrusion into their lives. As time went on, my barrage of questions became increasingly informed and were usually answered with respect, even if behind such answers lay bewilderment about why any seemingly intelligent person would collect such information.

Chapter 2

The Essential Context

Looking north from Stage Cove on a clear August day in 1980, my thoughts drifted to what history records is the importance of this place. Stage Cove, on the south side of the St. Charles River, is between Cape Charles and Lodge Bay, Labrador. Several kilometers to the northeast lay Great Caribou Island and Battle Harbour, historic center of the area, and directly behind me, the house remains of eighteenth-century English adventurer George Cartwright. My exploration of these ruins was suddenly interrupted by the arrival of a Cape Charles speedboat driven by Gus, a knowledgeable Lodge Bay elder. Once he joined me, Gus confidently pointed to a grassy mound and said "ol' Cartwright lived over there." After he disappeared behind a hummock in search of *bakeapples*, I resumed my exploration. Measuring the low mounds that had once been walls, I noted several pieces of thin bluish-green glass and a few square-headed nails. These were certainly old and consistent with what one would expect from a late eighteenth-century site. Cartwright's tenure in the area had been preceded by prehistoric aboriginal and European peoples. As I sat overlooking the bay, my mind drifted to the succession of peoples who had come to terms with Labrador's rigorous subarctic environment.

This chapter provides some temporal and spatial context for the ethnographic observations to follow, covering the natural environment, prehistory, and European history of the area. My account of the environment concentrates on four main environmental features that characterize the Lodge Bay and Cape Charles area: the consequences of the ancient glaciers that once covered Labrador, the Labrador current, Labrador's two coastlines, and its periodic scarcity and abundance of natural resources.

During the two-million-year-long Pleistocene geological epoch, lasting until approximately 10,000 years before present (B.P.), most of the Quebec-Labrador peninsula lay covered by glaciers—immense layers of snow and ice one to two kilometers thick. Glaciation meant that brooks and rivers deposited less water into the sea, and consequently, sea levels, like temperatures, were lower than today's. Additionally, glaciers scoured the land bare of topsoil (depositing it well offshore), moved huge boulders onto barren uplands and gouged the surface of Labrador's Precambrian geology (granites and gneisses almost as old as the earth itself) producing a complex maze of rivers, fjords, and lakes. In short, the Pleistocene sculptured the Labrador landscape.

The second important environmental feature occurs in the form of an invisible yet dominating cold ocean flow, the infamous Labrador current. The Labrador current includes waters from two cold arctic currents and from the (relatively) warmer Irminger, or West Greenland, current. These three currents converge at the northernmost tip of Labrador (Cape Chidley) and flow southward. The Labrador current continuously veers landward, depositing its frozen cargo (pack ice from the Canadian arctic archipelago and towering icebergs that splinter off Greenland's ice cap each year) at protruding capes and headlands. Along with the climatic consequences of prevailing continental air masses that continually flow just south of the region, the Labrador current chills air temperatures, ensuring long, cold winters and short summers. The frigid effect of the icy waters (though technically subarctic) of the Labrador current on climate is underscored by comparison: Lodge Bay lies on about the same parallel north latitude as Amsterdam, Holland, yet few tulips color Labrador springs!

The mixing of the cold and salty waters of the Labrador current with those of the warmer Gulf Stream (occurring off much of eastern Newfoundland and southern Labrador) has two other effects on the Lodge Bay region: it enriches all marine life, and causes considerable precipitation, notably fog during early summer.

As A. Prince Dyke (1969, 128) observed, Labrador essentially has two coastlines—an inner or mainland coast of sheltered bays and inlets, and an outer coast of barren capes and islands. The climate of the exposed outer coast is marine—variable but normally raw and damp. That of the inner coast is continental, stable, drier, and extreme; quite hot in summer and cold in winter. The natural resources of both coasts differ substantially. Historically, the outer coast has been the ocean breadbasket while the inner coast includes boreal forest flora and fauna. There is an essential symbiosis, an interdependency, between these two coasts. People need the forest resources of the inner coast to procure the marine resources of the outer coast, and vice versa. This symbiosis underwrites an ancient settlement pattern that Dyke, borrowing the term *transhumance* from geographic work elsewhere, called *seasonal transhumance*. People moved seasonally, inhabiting sheltered bays in winter and exposed islands and headlands in summer.

Finally, seasonal and periodic resource scarcity and abundance have had an immense influence on Labrador people such as the Settlers of Lodge Bay. Unlike more temperate and naturally diverse environments, where a great many species inhabit an area for a greater portion of each year, the number of species found in Labrador is rather small; most are seasonal residents, using the area for only part of their annual cycle. Fortunately for people, not all of these transient species visit during the same time of year and, when visiting, do so in great numbers. Both the strength and vulnerability of this small inventory of transient species continues to be its seasonal and cyclic availability: its periodic scarcity or abundance.

When discussing the proportion of resident to migratory species in northern Labrador, Vaino Tanner (1944, 430) notes that only 10 percent of the approximately 225 species of birds are year-round residents. The scarcity of resident species meant that one key to human adaptation was successful exploitation of the visitors. These passed by in great numbers seasonally, particularly in fall, spring, and summer. Each October and November Labrador skies blackened with millions of common eider, harlequin, and oldsquaw ducks flying south. A little later, enormous pods (herds) of harp seals also headed south to give birth, ideally passing Cape Charles just before the sea ice froze fast to the land and people retreated from the barren headlands and islands to the shelter of Lodge Bay. Spring brought back the same transients, waterfowl and seals, this time migrating northward. Settlers traveled to the outer coast to harvest them and soon thereafter the next visitors, Atlantic salmon, made their appearance. Salmon were followed by three more transient fish species: caplin, the diminutive ecological base of the marine ecosystem; cod, the economic mainstay; and then herring, the occasionally significant alternative. Large and small marine mammals entered southeastern Labrador waters by late summer and some remained for several months. By late fall, the seasonal cycle of transients began again.

If one key to human habitation lay in exploiting transient species in fall, spring, and summer, the other lay in effective use of boreal forest resources during winter. Some of the latter were residents, most obviously coniferous trees like the important black (and less important white) spruce and balsam fir comprising the boreal forest, as well as a handful of deciduous trees, such as birch. Other resident flora, some found along the outer coast, lay covered by snow in winter and were therefore gathered during other times of the year. I am thinking here of vascular plants, such as *bog bean*, a green and sour-tasting marsh plant Lodge Bay people used as a medicine, as well as better known grasses, lichens, and berrying plants. Finally, a variety of other species found in or near the boreal forest, including bear, hares, ptarmigan, grouse, and various species of fur-bearing animals—to list a few—all provided Lodge Bay people with food or furs.

Prehistory

Considerable archaeological research on Labrador prehistory has taken place over the past two decades. Archaeological analysis of surviving stone and bone tools, radiocarbon dates, dwellings, and burials has produced a chronology of five major prehistoric traditions. Most archaeological research has occurred in the Strait of Belle Isle, Lake Melville, and northern Labrador. Until recently, the southeastern Labrador coast was an archaeological enigma. However, the archaeological surveys of Marianne Stopp and Doug Rutherford (1991) and Stopp and Ken Reynolds (1992), shed much-needed light on the area. In 1991 Stopp and Rutherford surveyed the coast between Cape Charles and Seal Island and then in 1992 Stopp and Reynolds surveyed the coast between Frenchmen's Island and Trunmore Bay.

Around 10,000 years ago the glaciers began to melt and sea levels rose at the rate of about 30 centimeters per century. Rivers flowed again and forests and other vegetation began to grow. Deglaciation had begun. These and other climatic and ecological changes gradually created an environment suitable for people.

The earliest people to inhabit Labrador arrived in the Strait of Belle Isle around 9000 B.P. Archaeologists call them Palaeo-Indians. They did not remain in Labrador long, appear not to have moved north of the Strait, and left few remains. About 8500 B.P. (Tuck 1982, 205) the so-called Maritime Archaic tradition emerged. Maritime Archaic peoples remained in Labrador for approximately 5,000 years, moving as far north as the Saglek area. Their tool inventory included ground slate adzes and gouges, suggesting an emphasis on woodworking, and bone harpoon heads, indicating a dependence on marine resources, an assumption supported by the discovery of seal and waterfowl bones at Maritime Archaic sites. The presence of caribou bones hints that these early people also used interior resources. Although Stopp et al. do not identify any Maritime Archaic sites from Cape Charles, a Lodge Bay man showed me a spear point (made from white quartile or chert) that locals found while building a foot path high above Injun Cove, Cape Charles, in the mid-1970s. My photograph of the projectile point enabled Memorial University archaeologists to identify it as Maritime Archaic.

Around 4,000 years ago, Maritime Archaic peoples who had moved north to Saglek Bay, apparently met and were gradually replaced by the first of two prehistoric Inuit-like peoples, whom archaeologists call the Early Palaeo- (or old) Eskimos. Palaeo-Eskimos entered Labrador from the north, and at Saglek, where their cultural remains lie directly above those of the Maritime Archaic, there is some evidence of trade between these two peoples (Tuck 1975).

Small microlithic chert tools, probably tied to wooden handles or arrow shafts, are common to Palaeo-Eskimo tool kits. In southeastern Labrador, as across the arctic, Early Palaeo-Eskimo sites are commonly located near the marine resources that constituted the focus of their adaptation. Stopp et al. noted two early Palaeo-Eskimo sites during their 1991 survey—both of the "Groswater Sequence"—one located north of Cape Charles at Square Islands and the other south, near Camp Islands.

A second, more recent prehistoric Eskimo-like tradition found in Labrador is the Late Palaeo-Eskimo or Dorset, which dates from approximately 2500 to 1800 B.P. and is often divided into smaller sequential stages (Early, Middle, and Late Dorset). Like the Early Palaeo-Eskimo tradition, the Dorset ranged across the entire Canadian arctic. Dorset artifacts include small, delicate tools, and sculptured animal figurines (perhaps used as ritual amulets). The large number of Dorset sites attests to their successful adaptation. Stopp and her associates found twenty-seven Dorset sites during the summers of 1991 and 1992; most of the so-called Middle Dorset period and found along the coast north of Cape Charles.

Labrador's final prehistoric tradition, the so-called Thule or neo-Eskimo, spans the border between history and prehistory. The Thule tradition originated in Alaska around A.D. 1000. Thule peoples later migrated eastward across the Canadian arctic, reaching Labrador around A.D. 1400, four centuries after Norse adventurers visited the region and only a century or so before the earliest European fishers and whalers. While the Thule tradition is the best known of the five prehistoric periods discussed—partic-ularly from Groswater Bay north—positive identification of Thule sites is complicated in southeastern Labrador by the arrival of transient European fishers, who built sod houses that are today very difficult to distinguish from Thule sod houses (Auger 1991). Consequently, while we know Labrador Inuit inhabited south-eastern Labrador during the nineteenth century, the trail of their late Thule ancestors is less known.

Though Labrador prehistory is still shrouded in the conundrums unavoidable in the study of archaeology, the lesson from what we do know is the necessity of a seasonal adaptation to the Labrador environment. Peoples inhabiting southeastern Labrador prior to recorded time moved to exploit seasonally available resources. When times were good, such as after many animals, fish, or birds had been killed, prehistoric peoples congregated briefly in larger numbers, as if to test but quickly confirm the demographic limits of their mobile hunting and gathering economy.

Historic Aboriginal Peoples

During historic times, the area around Lodge Bay and Cape Charles was occasionally occupied by Labrador's two aboriginal peoples, the Inuit (previously called Eskimos) and the Innu (or Indians). Each summer Inuit traders were drawn south to the Strait of Belle Isle to trade with transient Europeans. Most Inuit, however, appear to have returned to the northern Labrador coast each fall to trade treasured European goods with more isolated Inuit groups. Like their prehistoric Thule ancestors, historic Inuit spoke Inuktitut and referred to one another as Inuit, meaning the "real" or "true" people. Their nomadic hunting, foraging, and fishing economy focused on hunting marine animals, notably baleen whale species; on fishing for salmon and arctic char; and on foraging for a variety of foods, ranging from seaweeds to berries. Inuit technology was subtly intricate and portable, consistent with their flexible and nomadic lifestyle. They made clothing from seal and caribou skins; knives, harpoon heads, and arrow points from bone or stone; and lamps and cooking vessels from soapstone. Sealskin tents, sod and whalebone semisubterranean houses, and snow houses provided shelter. Unlike the earlier Dorset peoples, Thule and historic Inuit used dogs to pull long wooden sleds (komatiks) and, in summer, used skin-covered *kayaks* and *umiaks* (women's boats) for sea transportation and hunting. Social organization included small kin-based groups that customarily exploited particular regions of the coast. Several such groups commonly congregated for a few weeks each summer at a favorite bay or island. There, they exchanged news and renewed intergroup alliances through the mechanisms of marriage, trade, and ritual. Contact between Inuit traders visiting the Cape Charles area and early Europeans was sometimes hostile, though progressively less so after the British takeover in 1763.

Present-day Labrador Innu (Naskapi and/or Montagnais Indians) practice a nomadic hunting culture perhaps dating back to the Maritime Archaic times. While the anthropological stereotype of the Innu is of nomadic caribou hunters of the barren Labrador interior, their late prehistoric ancestors likely spent more time on the coast (Loring 1992), practicing a more generalized adaptation, perhaps like their Algonkian relatives in the Canadian Maritimes. The arrival of the Europeans displaced Innu from the coast, just as the fur trade would later transform their economy.

Early European History

Early European exploitation of what is now Newfoundland and Labrador began around A.D. 1000, when Greenlandic Norse adventurers spent one or more winters at L'Anse aux Meadows, in northern Newfoundland.

Over 400 years later, in 1497, Giovanni Caboto (John Cabot), sailed to Newfoundland and, possibly, to Labrador. Cabot was followed by other European voyages of discovery, fishing, and whaling, gradually accumulating knowledge of the contours of the southern Labrador coastline. Early European opinions of Labrador—such as the note on the Ribero map of 1529 that there was "nothing of much value" in Labrador or Jacques Cartier's 1534 condemnation that Labrador (actually, the Quebec North Shore) was the "land God gave to Cain"—were soon followed by increased European exploitation of the "new lands." After about 1500, Europeans fished in the Strait of Belle Isle, and between 1550 and 1600 the Spanish Basques conducted a seasonal whale hunt in the Strait of Belle Isle, ranging as far north as Cape Charles. Next came the fur trade, colonization of New France (most of eastern North America), and numerous European explorations along the Labrador coast in search of a northwest route to the orient.

The French Regime

Until the 1660s, most French colonization took place in what is now Quebec. Much of this was in the Quebec interior and undertaken by traders licensed by the French Crown. Those holding so-called seigniorial land concessions were particularly interested in netting migrating pods of adolescent and adult harp seals each fall and spring. The French Crown also granted concessionaires exclusive rights to hunt, fish, and trade with aboriginal peoples. Some seigniorial concessions were made in perpetuity, but most were restricted to nine or ten years, stipulating that the concession-aire occupy and use the rights granted and pay annual dues (rent), normally several beaver skins, to the Crown.

By the 1660s, the French extended the seigniorial system to the north shore of the Gulf of St. Lawrence, the Strait of Belle Isle region, northern Newfoundland, and ultimately, southeastern Labrador. The first seigniorial concession to portions of southeastern Labrador was awarded in 1702 to Augustin Legardeur, Seigneur de Courtemanche. He obtained a ten-year trading grant from the Governor of New France for the coast between the Kegaska River (near Anticosti Island) and the Kessessasskiou River (now Churchill River). Courtemanche established an impressive headquarters, ultimately numbering some 200 buildings, at Bradore, Quebec.

In 1735 Governor C. Marquis de Beauharnois and Gilles Hocquart, civil administrator of New France, granted permission to Antoine Marsal, a Quebec City trader, to establish a sealing and trading post at Cape Charles. Marsal's initial Cape Charles concession ran from 1735 to 1744 and extended from Cape Charles to the "bay commonly called St. Alexis," showing that some contemporary place names were already in use (Beauharnois and Hocquart 1735).

Inuit attacked Marsal's Cape Charles post in 1742, and heavy ice conditions during the unusually severe winter of 1742–43 carried away all his seal nets. Louis Fornel's (1742) description of the Inuit attack on Marsal's post states that some of Marsal's men had "imprudently fired at [Inuit] in order to drive them away from an island where they had built huts." This precipitated the attack, which occurred in spring or early summer 1742. Marsal's post was burned, sacked and looted; the boats he had constructed were destroyed; and two of his three men who garrisoned the post were killed. Consequently, in 1743, Marsal could not recruit workers for the post and had to abandon some of his fishing gear near the Cape (Beauharnois and Hocquart 1743).

Following these setbacks, Marsal risked everything by borrowing money from friends and applying for and receiving a six-year extension to his Cape Charles concession. However, for unknown reasons, Marsal's affairs "compelled him to return to France" (Duquesne and Bigot 1753), and he did not use his new lease to Cape Charles. The assumed economic potential of Cape Charles was not to be ignored for long. In 1749, a M. Baune (or de Bonne), described as a "half-pay Captain" in the Conde infantry regiment, received a nine-year lease (Lajonquiere and Bigot 1749). However, it appears that Captain Baune never sent anyone to operate the Cape Charles post and returned his patent. But Marsal soon returned. In 1751, his concession for Petit Havre (probably the Petty Harbour north of St. Lewis) took effect and, in 1753, he requested and received permission for "another attempt" at Cape Charles (Duquesne and Bigot 1753).

Marsal's new grant for Cape Charles was to run from 1754 to 1763 and, even though he died in 1757, his name continued to be associated with Cape Charles. Thus, in 1758, Marsal's creditors united under the name of Tachet and applied for a nine-year lease to Marsal's Cape Charles post, so as to recover the 7,000 livres they had advanced him. In their petition, Tachet and the others noted that Marsal had done a "considerable amount of work in connection with that post and its fitting up" and, in using their funds, had "so often held out the expectation of profits" (Tachet et al. 1758). While Marsal's creditors received permission to operate the post, it is not known whether they succeeded in recovering their losses.

The significance of the French regime lies in the fact that following the Basques, the French were the first Europeans to systematically exploit the coast north of the Labrador Strait region (Trudel 1978). Whether the French system of exploitation—Crown-leased concessions—was the most efficient method is debatable, though repeated applications for places such as Cape Charles suggest that the potential was considered tremendous. Patricia Thornton (1977, 155) and Stopp and Rutherford (1991, 32) mention another legacy of the French regime. Both in the Strait and southeastern Labrador regions, British adventurers and permanent Settlers reused locations discovered and used earlier by French concessioners. Thus, except for the brief and little-known period between 1775 and 1830, Cape Charles was used continuously as a whaling, sealing, and fishing settlement as far back as Marsal's initial grant (1735). Similarly, the site of the contemporary winter community of Lodge Bay was utilized by Marsal, Nicholas Darby, Captain Cartwright, and the ancestors of contemporary folk. Thus, the French initiated European exploration of southeastern Labrador and established precedents followed after the fall of New France in 1763.

Captain Cartwright and the Early British Era

Following the British defeat of the French in North America (1760) and the resulting Treaty of Paris (1763), the administration of coastal Labrador was located in St. John's, Newfoundland. Early British colonial policy and use of coastal Labrador contrasted with that during the French regime. Labrador was to be used primarily for a summer cod fishery; permanent settlement by British colonists was discouraged. Such policies kept control of the fishery in the hands of powerful West English merchants and sought to train young fishers for eventual service in His Majesty's Navy. However, such limited use of Labrador prevented the exploitation of valuable Labrador resources, particularly furs and seals, which had to be taken in the fall and winter. Consequently, the early British policies would eventually be ignored. Our window into the early British era comes largely from the three-volume diary of a British adventurer, Captain George Cartwright, who, coincidentally, began his sixteen-year-long Labrador career at Cape Charles and Lodge Bay.

In 1770 Captain Cartwright in collaboration with three partners sailed to Labrador and took possession of a house formerly occupied by Nicholas Darby, an earlier English adventurer, on the north side of the St. Charles River. Ranger Lodge, as Cartwright named the site (after His Majesty's schooner, the *Ranger*), would become his first winter headquarters and, like the summer post he claimed at Cape Charles, was used by Marsal as early as 1735. Cartwright and his men trapped furs, netted seals and salmon, and hunted in the area between Chateau Bay and St. Lewis Inlet. Just as contemporary Settlers do, Cartwright wintered at Ranger Lodge and lived at Cape Charles during the open water season.

Cartwright's salmon post at Ranger Lodge was raided in June 1772 by the larger and more powerful rival firm of Noble and Pinson, initiating a fierce competition that dogged Cartwight until he left Labrador in 1786. The raids inspired Cartwright's important Memorial, delivered to the British government in 1773, which stressed the need for year-round residence and permanent ownership of salmon and sealing *berths*. Beginning in 1773, Cartwright expanded north to Sandwich Bay, establishing Caribou Castle as his winter headquarters in 1775, salmon posts at all major rivers emptying into Sandwich Bay, and a codfishing station at Great Island (now Cartwright Island). During the American Revolution, Cartwright's Sandwich Bay posts were raided by Boston privateer John Grimes, leading to Cartwright's eventual bankruptcy in 1785 and final exodus from Labrador in 1786.

The significance of Cartwright is that his argument for year-round settlement of Labrador eventually prevailed, paving the way for early settlement; that he practiced seasonal transhumance at Lodge Bay and Cape Charles; and that his diary provides an indispensable impression of life during the early British era.

Little is known about the period following Cartwright's exodus from Labrador, in 1786, until the 1830s, an unfortunate loss because this is when permanent European colonialization occurred. How did early settlement occur? Who were the first settlers, and how did they gain a foothold in Labrador?

Cartwright and other early English merchants hired servants for stints of two summers and a winter, providing living expenses and annually paying wages for labor. Servants were exclusively young men; most came from the interior of West England; and many were former farmhands or tradesmen displaced by agricultural or industrial change. Some servants remained in Labrador for several years and eventually settled on their own drawing essential supplies from their former employers. As explained elsewhere (Kennedy 1995), this transition was complicated by competition between British merchants for servants. Moreover, some evidence suggests that merchants considered independent settlers a threat to their exploitation of local resources. Coincidentally, the large United States fishing fleet that began to fish in Labrador in the late 1700s, brought with it illicit trade both with servants who were attempting to become independent settlers and their former employers, the British merchants. It appears that such trade created the free market necessary for former servants-turned-settlers to survive. These settlers obtained some supplies from local merchants but also traded some of their produce with transient fishers from the New England coast.

Although servants eventually became permanent Settlers, few details of this process, survive. Moreover, little information exists on the early years of the historic Settler lifestyle, and this is especially true of their lives during winter. Once families left the outer coast each fall for their winter quarters, it was as if they became invisible, truly people without a history. No chroniclers, like de Tocqueville, wintered among the Settlers. They wintered beyond the fringes of literature or time. We have only glimpses of their winter lifestyle, sketched out on the coast by lettered summertime visitors, like H. C. Walsh (1896) and Charles Townsend (1907), who jotted a few lines about Labrador's permanent residents. After all, compared to the Newfoundland fishers who, during the 1900s, would flood the Labrador coast each summer, the Settlers were an insignificant minority, a few families whose pioneering lifestyle was an anachronism.

The 1832 Moss Diary is a rare exception, providing a brief account of early nineteenth-century Battle Harbour. It contains the earliest reference to the most common contemporary surname in Lodge Bay, Battle Harbour servant W. Pye. We must assume that W. Pye is related, perhaps as father, to James Pye (1830–93), the earliest Pye listed in the Battle Harbour church records (which begin in 1850) and more certainly to the Pyes described by late nineteenth-century summer visitors.

Such visitors provide priceless snapshots of this seasonal community. Walsh's (1896, 33) book, for example, contains a photograph of a Cape Charles family and describes the community in July 1894, as consisting of "a half-dozen families" who would "take to the woods" each winter (i.e., go to Lodge Bay). Townsend (1907) visited Cape Charles in July 1906 and adds more details: there were sixteen families, and Settlers moved to Cape Charles in March and to Lodge Bay in October. Moreover, one of Townsend's photos depicts some of the same stages and fish stores still used in 1979. The Reverend P. W. Browne's visit to Cape Charles (apparently in 1891) suggests the antiquity of other contemporary patterns, including English pronunciation. Thus, Browne (1909, 233) describes the curiosity of Injun Cove Pyes surrounding his visit and their discovery that his "'twas the *clargy*'s boat."

The accounts of Walsh, Townsend, Browne, and other visitors describe a remarkably persistent lifestyle. While the Pyes and other families wintering at Lodge Bay appear to have changed little between the nineteenth and twentieth centuries, events and policies originating beyond Labrador would eventually entangle Lodge Bay.

On the heels of the American (and French) Labrador fishery came the important Newfoundland fishery. Each spring, floater crews (so called because the fishing schooners moved from place to place) primarily from Newfoundland's Conception Bay sailed to Labrador to fish for cod and transport their salted catches home to Newfoundland. Another Newfoundland fishery along coastal Labrador, the stationers, journeyed to Labrador aboard coasting vessels and fished in small boats from their fishing stations. Stationers included whole families (plus some domesticated livestock), who owned *rooms* along the Labrador coast and often stored their fishing boats and gear over winter in Labrador. Newfoundland fishers were extremely important to Settlers at places like Cape Charles. Each summer's arrival from Newfoundland brought people, information, new ideas, and developed strong ties between Labrador and Newfoundland communities. Stationers and floaters from Carbonear and Harbour Grace (both in Conception Bay) fished around Cape Charles and created links between the people of both places. Such ties were

Ephrain Pye and family. Cape Charles, c. 1905. (Photograph courtesy of Mr. and Mrs. Paul Pye)

further strengthened when young Conception Bay people married Cape Charles spouses, creating affinal ties; this then meant that Conception Bay became the destination for occasional fall or winter visits by Lodge Bay residents.

Early in the twentieth century, Lodge Bay men worked some autumns in the herring fishery on Newfoundland's west coast, especially in the Bay of Islands and later, in the nearby Corner Brook paper mill. Access to Newfoundland's west coast was facilitated by coastal vessels that ran between Humbermouth (Corner Brook) and Battle Harbour (Labrador). Bonds between Cape Charles and Corner Brook, like those with Conception Bay communities, survive today.

Family-based codfishing crew, father (center) and two sons, at Wall's Tickle, Cape Charles, c. 1940. Note fish store in background, *handbarrow* in foreground, and oilskins on the two sons. (Photograph courtesy of Verna Pye)

Although relations between Labrador Settlers and their counterparts on the Island of Newfoundland were generally good, it is equally clear that successive Newfoundland governments (and in some instances, Newfoundlanders themselves) viewed Labrador and its people with ambivalence. On the one hand, the ice-bound and barren coast of Labrador was the place Newfoundland-based crews ventured each summer to fish; on the other hand, some Newfoundlanders considered Labrador people as the primitive Other, an impoverished folk whom they preferred to see as unlike themselves.

Certain facts document Labrador's subordinate relationship to island Newfoundland. Between 1809 (when Newfoundland resumed administration of coastal Labrador) and 1946, Newfoundland chose several times to deny the franchise to Labrador residents, even though Island Newfoundlanders were able to vote after 1832. Also, the government of Newfoundland attempted to lease or sell Labrador several times during this same period, notably after the

British Privy Council confirmed Newfoundland's position regarding the western and southern boundaries of its Labrador dependency. However, Newfoundland's government collected taxes and revenues from Labrador residents and merchants throughout this period; yet its services (seasonal schools, some welfare, periodic visits by government doctors, and telegraph stations) were minimal and unabashedly intended, at least primarily, to serve seasonal Newfoundland fishers. An anonymous report from 1920 records systemic injustices inflicted on Settlers by visiting fishers and by the "little army of government officials" who briefly visited the coast each summer. Even though Newfoundland governments have long considered Labrador its dependency, a place to be exploited, the people of Newfoundland and coastal Labrador generally enjoy a more evenhanded relationship, buttressed by ties of kinship and marriage.

As noted above, the history of Lodge Bay is dominated by persistence, twice-a-year transhumant moves, and resource use, associated with Labrador's inner and outer coast. The community has maintained a relatively stable size during much of the past century. Thus, the Newfoundland census of 1874 lists Cape Charles's population as 58. By 1911, the population was 97, 106 by 1921, and 60 in 1935 (for further discussion of population trends, see chapter 6). Despite this relative persistence of lifestyle and scale, a number of changes have occurred and may be discussed in rough chronological order.

Between 1860 and 1880, a herring fishing boom occurred in the Cape Charles area, especially just north at Azzize's Harbour. This boom attracted fishers from Nova Scotia, the United States, Quebec, and other places and often exploded into conflict. A second herring boom occurred between the 1930s and 1950s, prompting Russian immigrant Francis Banikhin to establish a herring processing plant on Banikhin's Island, Cape Charles, in 1937. Banikhin employed local fishers on a part-time basis and is still remembered by older people.

In 1892, British medical missionary Dr. Wilfred Grenfell came to Newfoundland and Labrador and the following year opened his first hospital at Battle Harbour, then hub of Newfoundland's Labrador fishery, about six kilometers north of Cape Charles. The Grenfell Mission would develop into a major service administration, responsible for health care in much of northern Newfoundland and Labrador. In addition to health care, the Grenfell Mission promoted economic development, education, and agriculture. In 1916, for example, the Mission established a co-operative store at Cape Charles, apparently under the name of the Labrador Stores Ltd.

During the second decade of this century, the Mission, by then the International Grenfell Association (IGA), began to build hospitals to serve Settlers near their winter homes. The IGA chose Hatter's Cove, for example, as its winter hospital for Battle Harbour, and Lodge Bay carpenters helped build the Hatter's cove facility. In 1930, St. Mary's River (Mary's Harbour) replaced Hatter's Cove as Battle Harbour's new winter hospital site and would become the center for communities from Henley Harbour to St. Lewis (Fox Harbour). Significantly then, many of the Mission's policies required the centralization of people to Grenfell centers.

Labrador's modern whaling era began during the early years of this century. From about 1904 to 1912, Bowring Brothers of St. John's, merchants who supplied the Carbonear-based fishing fleet bound annually for Cape Charles, opened a whaling factory at Antle's Cove, roughly four kilometers west of Injun Cove, Cape Charles. While few locals were involved in the whaling enterprise, Pye brothers William and Albert served as winter caretakers and William's daughter Amelia married an employee of the factory.

In 1909, a group of London capitalists known as the Syndicate proposed a railway from central Canada to Cape Charles with the goal of reducing travel time between England and central Canada. The Syndicate proposed other schemes, including a ten- mile dam across the Strait of Belle Isle, topped by a rail line. By blocking the icy Labrador current, the dam would moderate weather conditions along the Atlantic coasts of Canada and the United States. Had the Syndicate's plans not been eventually abandoned, they would have profoundly affected Cape Charles, Lodge Bay, and the entire region.

A 1911 amendment to Newfoundland's Crown Lands Act initiated a flurry of timber concessions (though little actual cutting), just north of Lodge Bay. In 1934, Welsh entrepreneur J. O. Williams began a woods operation on the Alexis River, about forty kilometers north of Lodge Bay. Williams's Labrador Development Company (LDC) founded Port Hope Simpson, Labrador's first modern company town, and the company operated intermittently until the late 1940s. While some Lodge Bay men worked periodically cutting timber for the LDC, none moved to Port Hope Simpson.

In 1941, construction began on the massive military air base at Goose Bay, in Central Labrador. Lured by high wages, some Lodge Bay men worked a winter or two at Goose Bay, but unlike people from Sandwich Bay to Hopedale, few moved to Goose Bay permanently. Beginning in 1942, a few Lodge Bay men helped construct the wartime navigational station at White Point, about four kilometers north of Cape Charles; three men still worked there in 1979.

Following World War II, Great Britain pondered the future of its oldest colony, Newfoundland, which it had placed under an appointed Commission of Government in 1934. In 1945 British Prime Minister Clement Attlee announced a National Convention to consider Newfoundland's future. The National Convention chose to hold a referendum on whether Newfoundland and Labrador should vote to join the Canadian federation. Two ballots were necessary to secure a majority favoring confederation. Confederation took effect on 1 April 1949.

Confederation entitled residents of Canada's tenth province to the fruits of the emerging Canadian welfare state, including family allowances, old age security, universal health benefits, unemployment insurance benefits, and others. But there were also costs. Chief amongst these was loss of control over the offshore fishery, surrendered to Canada under the Terms of Union. And another was resettlement. The immense cost of providing newly acquired universal services to a dispersed population (415,000 in 1956, 90 percent of whom lived in some 3,000 tiny villages scattered along 6,000 miles of rugged coastline [Fraser 1958, 273–274]) did seem to necessitate some concentration of the population.

Resettlement programs began in the 1950s, initially requiring that 100 percent of a community's population vote to move. As successive resettlement programs were implemented, particularly as of 1965, policies allowed individual families to elect to move. Most government-assisted resettlement in southeastern Labrador occurred between 1967 and 1970. The communities of Cartwright and Mary's Harbour were enlarged with people from outlying communities, often creating enclaves within communities.

Lodge Bay resisted government pressures to resettle to nearby Mary's Harbour. Instead, Lodge Bay received several people from abandoned winter communities, primarily from Pitt's Arm. Significantly, communities like Lodge Bay, that chose not to move, were no larger nor more viable than those people abandoned. Instead, communities rejecting resettlement seem to have valued place and kin over the optimistic predictions of life in larger centers (Brox 1968).

Chapter 3

Making a Living

As with making a living elsewhere, the economy of Lodge Bay involves the production, distribution and exchange, and utilization of material things. Production, the first stage in the economic process, usually requires possession of the material things necessary to produce, social relationships with whom one produces, and the knowledge often necessary to know how to produce. The material things necessary to produce, or means to production, include use or ownership of salmon and cod fishing berths and boats, and the snowmobiles, sawmills, and traps used in winter.

Summer Economic Activities

Cape Charles fishers recognize local ownership of fishing berths, the favored locations where fishers set their nets for cod and salmon. Cape Charles berths are usually inherited through male kinship links. However, in the nearby community of St. Lewis (Fox Harbour), fishers draw for fishing berths before each season, ideally allowing all fishing crews equal chance for a good berth. St. Lewis fishers adopted this *harbor rule*, or lottery system about 1970 to avoid what had become a stampede by fishers to set nets and claim berths as soon as open water replaced sea ice. This frantic race had resulted in many nets being destroyed by icebergs or pack ice. In the 26 May 1979 lottery at St. Lewis, forty-seven prime salmon berths were drawn first, followed by the poorer quality berths. While such a system ensures all fishers a relatively equal share of prime, second, and poorer berths, the berths that one may draw can be located as much as sixteen to twenty kilometers apart, greatly increasing the time and expense of tending nets.

Aside from St. Lewis, most southeastern Labrador fishers, including those from Lodge Bay, inherit salmon and cod fishing berths and either inherit and/or purchase fishing gear. While definite rules for the acquisition of these means of production are unclear, there has been an emphasis toward agnatic descent— descent through male kinship ties. Other than that some variety existed. I recorded cases of partible and of impartible inheritance, of both ultimogeniture and primogeniture, and of female offspring (temporarily) inheriting fishing gear when there were no appropriate male heirs. And as elsewhere, the distribution of property some-times caused conflict. Many years ago, for example, Willis died, leaving to mourn his siblings Lorenzo and Susie. Seeing Lorenzo hauling away their dead brother's gear from his storehouse, Susie intervened, wanting her share. Battle Harbour Justice of the Peace Stan Brazil was called in to mediate, and Susie got her share of Willis's gear.

Other patterns related to the acquisition of property essential for fishing are more obvious. One of these is the developmental cycle of fishing crews, a phenomenon also described by Frank Southard (1982, 128–131). The oldest son begins fishing with his father, is later joined by his younger siblings, and assumes control of the crew once his father retires. Once the oldest son's children are in their teens, however, the sibling-based crew divides, with the oldest son assuming the status once occupied by his father. His younger brothers either continue to fish together or also become skippers, or leaders of crews composed primarily of their sons. This ideal pattern was observed in most Cape Charles fishing crews. It recruited labor necessary to fish using cod traps and, at least in principle, enabled a father to distribute berths and gear equitably among his sons. The developmental cycle of fishing crews was intrinsically related to the family and, depending on circumstances, either increased rivalry between brothers or reinforced the strength and solidarity of the family.

A second pattern found in Cape Charles involves cases in which younger siblings are unable to obtain berths and consequently are forced to purchase or otherwise acquire new berths and/or gear at new locations. This may be called the hiving-off pattern. An example of this pattern occurred in 1952 when a scarcity of *grounds* (that is, a shortage of fishing berths) caused two Cape Charles brothers (the two oldest) to leave their ancestral summer home at Waterin' Cove, Cape Charles, and begin fishing further south, at

Carrol's Cove. There, one of the brothers purchased a room from a Curling, Newfoundland, fisherman. In 1979, both brothers and their sons still fished at Carrol's Cove.

In other examples of hiving off among Cape Charles fishers, men began their fishing careers as boys at Cape Charles but were forced to move elsewhere to fish during their adult lives. Some of these men were able to return to fish at the Cape, however, once berths became available. The hiving-off principle is probably as old as permanent settlement itself (indeed, it indubitably caused the founding of many fishing stations) but has increased since about 1900, when Settlers began purchasing rooms from Newfoundland stationer fishers then abandoning the fishery.

Surprisingly, methods used by Cape Charles fishers to fish salmon, cod, and herring have changed relatively little during the past century, though some changes should be noted. Commercially produced nylon nets have replaced the older (but otherwise similar) hemp nets used in salmon fishing. Federal regulations, that specify how many running fathoms of net a fisher can fish at any one time, control fishing effort, especially in regard to the salmon fishery. Thus, while fishers possessing salmon licenses commonly own about 20 salmon nets, they may only be allowed to fish 400 fathoms, meaning they will use eight 50-fathom-long nets at a time. Their remaining nets may be temporarily ashore for mending and/or at some nearby stream for cleaning.

Salmon fishers must continuously clean green and viscous *slub* (plankton) from salmon nets. Slub makes the net visible to salmon, thus diminishing its fishing effectiveness. Fishers beat slub from nets using locally made *switches*. The nets are pulled across the gunwales of fishing boats and beaten with the switch. Nets hopelessly covered with slub may be placed in a freshwater stream where the current removes the slub. Cape Charles fishers maintain that the incidence of dirty water (slub) has increased since the 1960s. They claim that slub is more frequent during warm water conditions, such as during the middle of the salmon season. Finally, slub not only makes salmon nets visible to salmon but is also believed to deter cod from entering inshore waters.

Depending on local ice conditions, fishers set their salmon nets perpendicularly to the shoreline in late May or early June. In 1979, the first salmon was caught at Cape Charles on 1 June, though the first and main run of salmon usually begins about mid-June and lasts through early July. Two-man crews tend nets daily or, when salmon are plentiful, twice daily. Tending nets involves collecting salmon, setting or resetting nets, and the more tedious task of removing slub from the nets. Salmon are described as a *lee shore*

Men in motor or trap boat hauling cod trap. Cape Charles.

fish, and at Cape Charles the best catches are said to occur with easterly winds.

As happens, the 1979 salmon fishery was unsuccessful and fishers spent much of June doing other tasks. These included building or repairing wharfs and slipways, doing *twine work*, specifically sewing floors on cod traps, and dying trap nets dark brown, which is called "*barkin'* them."

The first signs of codfish appear in late June. In 1979, for example, fishers inadvertently took some cod in their salmon nets on 23 June. By this time each of Cape Charles's ten fishing crews had set one or more cod traps and had begun to take catches of one or two quintals. Local crews also make some use of commercially manufactured monofilament cod gill nets, which they set in late June. In 1979, as in several other southeastern Labrador communities, fishers from five Lodge Bay fishing crews paid approximately $4,000 for materials (nylon twine, lead sinkers, and cork floats) to construct five Japanese-style cod traps. An instructor from the Provincial College of Fisheries supervised the assembling of these cod traps in Lodge Bay. Fishers set the first of these traps at Cape Charles in late June.

Labor requirements for the short cod-trapping season are the

Fisher joyfully tossing
large codfish.
Cape Charles.

most extensive of any fishery, and crews may be augmented by local teenage boys on school holidays, and in some cases, by related women who help in gutting or heading codfish. Table 1 lists the size and social composition of Cape Charles's ten fishing crews. As can be seen, crews usually number about three related persons. These ten crews remained essentially unchanged in 1980.

Crews usually take their cod traps ashore about mid-August and then shift their fishing effort to the use of *gill nets*, baited longlines (locally called *trawls*), and/or *jiggers*. Cape Charles fisherman first used gill nets around 1965, when two brothers used them and caught about 200 quintals. However, gill nets are the least popular codfishing technology, and only certain crews use them. Like other fishers throughout Newfoundland and Labrador, Cape Charles fishers (including some who use gill nets) criticize gill nets for environmental reasons. Gill nets are said to catch the fat spawning fish, to drown fish caught in the net's mesh, thus lowering its quality, and, if lost from their moorings, to continue fishing in perpetuity, thereby killing a variety of species accidentally

Table 1 CAPE CHARLES FISHING CREWS, 1979		
Skipper	Crew Member(s)	Relationship to Skipper
Herb	Earl Rod	None; hired shareman None; hired shareman
Jim	Tom Sid	Brother Son
Walt	Dick Shawn	Son Son
Herman	Lester	Brother
Gus	John Tim	Son Son
Bob	Adrian	Brother-in-law
Greg	Andy Irving	Brother Brother
Bill	Louis Ford	Brother None; hired shareman
Peter	Joe Clyde	Son Son
Sam	Mark Dan	Son Son

entangled in what are appropriately called ghost nets. Even so, some Cape Charles crews used gill nets.

Cape Charles fishers have strong opinions about the effectiveness of particular fishing technologies and appropriate timing for their use. For example, some claim that you will not catch cod in gill nets when you are catching them on the *longline*; that you will not trap fish (in a cod trap) when you can jig them; that cod (and other species) cannot be caught during low tides; that if there is no snow on the land during winter, there will be no salmon or bakeapples, and so on. These beliefs support an ordered, proper, seasonal approach to fishing.

Longline hooks are baited with squid or herring and set on shoals or in deep water. The baited hooks run from meter-long *saidlines*, spaced about one meter apart along a *mainline* that sits on the ocean floor. Each end of the mainline is attached to a vertical *byline* extending up from the sea floor to surface buoys or floats. Hauling longlines requires the strong backs of two fishers. As each portion

Men pronging codfish from boat. Cape Charles.

Green cod or cod in bulk in fish store at Mattie's Cove. Handmade wheelbarrow in foreground.

of the longline is hauled, one fisher stands on one side of the boat taking fish off the hooks while the other stands on the opposite side, rebaiting the hooks and feeding the longline back into the water. Codfish caught by longline in autumn tend to be larger than *trap fish* and are called by names such as *deep water fish*, *herring fish*, or extra large *jowler* fish, the last because such fish are so big that the crew's *header* must cut around the lower jaw or jowls of the fish in order to rip off its head.

Regardless of whether cod are caught by trap, net, jigger, or longline, they are processed alike, using a timeless method once widespread throughout Newfoundland and Labrador. Crews arriving by boat to Cape Charles, like that of Jim, Tom, and Sid mentioned earlier, begin by using a two-pronged pitchfork to *prong* each fish onto the wharf or stage head. (To ensure a higher quality of fish, the use of fish prongs has been prohibited since the early 1980s.) Codfish are then pronged into a rectangular wooden box

Small codfish (winter fish) drying on flakes.
Cape Charles, 1980. ▶

located at one end of the splitting table to await processing. From there the crew, each member named for his role in the production process (header, splitter, salter), carries out a specific act on each fish, one cutting its throat and slitting its belly, another ripping off its head and removing the entrails, and another carefully splitting each fish and removing its backbone. Split fish are then washed in water and transported to the bulk. There they are stacked with their interiors lying up and beside one another, head to tail, on top of earlier catches, and heavily salted in tiered layers called bulks. Codfish absorb salt in bulk for a minimum of twenty-one days, after which they are *struck*. Struck fish are washed, scrubbed, and stacked in faggots or *waterhorses* to squeeze out any remaining water. When the weather is dry but not too sunny, fish are laid head to tail, either on wooden flakes or cobbled *bawn*, to dry. Each night crews or their families gather the drying fish, pile them in faggots, and cover them with canvas to reduce exposure to dampness. This process of drying salted codfish continues for a week or so, depending on drying conditions.

Older people fondly remember the traditional salt cod fishery. Women and children played important roles in the cutting of fish at the splitting tables and in helping to spread and stack drying fish. For wives and mothers otherwise confined to tedious household duties inside, the time outdoors spreading codfish on flakes or bawns was a welcome change.

Local crews catch herring in August and September, in gill nets. Fishers process herring by heading and then removing the *gibs* (gills and entrails) and *pip* (entrails and air sack).

Hand barrel.
Cape Charles.

Exchange and Utilization in the Fishery

Cape Charles fishers sell their salmon and cod differently. Cod is sold to only one buyer, salmon to several buyers. Salt codfish is a heavy product and the Canadian Salt Fish Corporation establishes prices prior to each season. Cape Charles fishers produce all their codfish in salt bulk, that is, split, salted, and layered in bulks. All this fish is eventually marketed through the Canadian Salt Fish Corporation, a Crown Corporation established by the federal government in 1970 to "improve the earnings of the primary producers of cured codfish" in Newfoundland and Labrador and along the North Shore of Quebec (Canadian Salt Fish Corporation 1981, 1). The corporation purchases fish only through its licensed agents.

The agent closest to Cape Charles is Earle Freighting Service at Battle Harbour. Earle Brothers of Carbonear, Newfoundland,

Grading salt bulk fish at Cape Charles fish store. Employee of Earle Freighting Service to right; Cape Charles fisher to left.

purchased the old Baine Johnston premises at Battle Harbour in 1955 and began buying *green* codfish. Each fall Earle's boats collect salt bulk cod at Cape Charles and other fishing stations. The fish is graded, shipped to Battle Harbour, and then sent to drying plants in Conception Bay, Newfoundland.

Though little survives of the monopolistic control merchants once held over fishers, I observed one incident that I consider a vestige of that era. In early June 1979, I accompanied two Cape Charles fishers to Battle Harbour. The Earle Brothers agent directed us into his office where a brief and good-natured conversation ensued. The agent then produced a bottle of liquor and poured all a drink. While not wanting to exaggerate what may have only been an innocuous and brief imbibe, the agent's offering seemed to me to be a ritual invitation symbolizing the commencement of that year's obligations, which merchants expected from fishers.

Cape Charles fishers sell a portion of their salmon catches to various resident and traveling buyers, primarily to increase competition and prices. Fresh chilled salmon are more transportable and more valuable than cod, and salmon prices are primarily regulated by market forces, a situation contrasting with cod prices, which are established by the Salt Fish Corporation. Although there is some risk in selling salmon to transient buyers (who, in the past, occasionally cheated fishers), all realize that multiple buyers raise prices. At the same time, fishers express some loyalty to their suppliers, notably Earle Brothers, a fact illustrated during the temporary price wars paid for salmon in late June 1979. Cape Charles fishers saved some of their salmon to sell to Earle Brothers, even though one of the two other salmon buyers offered a better price (prices ranged between $2 and $2.20 per pound). On the one hand, fishers appreciated the risk inherent in Earle's Battle Harbour operation and very much wanted the company to continue there; but on the other hand, fishers continued to sell some of their salmon for higher prices to transient buyers, perhaps motivated by convenience or the higher price paid. It is my impression that the extent to which fishers sell to multiple buyers differs from one community to another. Cape Charles fishers may represent the more independent end of a dependency continuum, while fishers from other communities are less willing to risk the wrath of merchant pressures to trade only with them. In the years before the standardization of cod prices, Cape Charles fishers occasionally withheld their codfish, waiting for a better price. Oral tradition includes stories of local fishers threatening burly fish buyers when they considered the prices they offered to be too low.

The practice of fishers selling fish to buyers other than the merchant who supplied them provisions on credit may be called leakage. In my view, leakage has been a continuous though underreported characteristic of Newfoundland and Labrador economic history, even though the potential and the reasons for leakage vary over time. Certainly economic possibilities of Battle Harbour area fishers were more open, though limited, than the closed system described by Sean Cadigan (1990). Thus, while Cape Charles fishers were under the watchful eye of their suppliers at Battle Harbour (Baine Johnston and Co.), older Settlers recalled clandestine trips to Blanc Sablon Quebec to purchase cheaper flour and tobacco. They also recall splitting their sales of codfish between Baine Johnston (Battle Harbour) and Soper at Cape Charles. Their motivation then was competition and prices, while today the motivation has to do with the unemployment insurance (UI) system.

In 1979 Cape Charles herring fishers sold their catch to Cabot Stores, a Labrador Strait firm that leased the community-owned fish holding plant and hired a local man to supervise the collection of herring. Fishers cleaned and salted their herring round (i.e., whole, but headless and gutless) in 45-gallon plastic drums and later shipped them out for secondary processing.

The proceeds of salmon, cod, and herring sales constitute the major method of generating cash in the Lodge Bay–Cape Charles economy. The survival of the credit system means that locals use their fishing incomes to repay goods obtained on credit; this especially applies to transactions with Earle Freighting Service. As importantly, fishers collect UI *stamps* (insurable week) for each week they fish, by selling fish to buyers.

While fishers sell most of their catch, fish remains an important staple in the local diet. Locals consume some fresh fish during summer and preserve some for later consumption by smoking or bottling. Other species associated with the outer coast form an important part of the summer diet, including mussels, mackerel, sea trout, seal, and dolphin.

Vegetables and fruit either grown or consumed at Cape Charles include locally grown *greens* (notably immature cabbage and young turnip tops), rhubarb, wild greens such as Alexander (*Ligusticum scothicum L.*), and berries, principally bakeapples.

In the past, people also used local plants for medicinal purposes. In 1979, these were less used; the plant names that I collected were given to me by older people. As elsewhere in Labrador (Goudie 1973, 11), spring tonics were made from boiled spruce or juniper boughs, along with other ingredients. The Moss diary entry for 9 May records going to Caribou Island for ''spruce to brew with'' (1832, 9). The tonic was made by boiling black spruce branches and then draining the liquid into a jar. Molasses or sugar and yeast were then added and the resulting concoction brewed for 10 to 12 days. The tonic or *spruce beer* served as a purgative, to "clean the blood" and to prevent colds after the long winter. Later, spruce beer was used as an alcoholic beverage. Tonics were also made from other plants. Colds, stomach pains, and menstrual cramps were treated with a tonic made from *ground juniper*. Boiled ground juniper was also given to babies "to make them healthy." Another blood-cleaning medicine was made with a spoonful each of molasses and sulphur.

Balsam fir *bladders* (whose contents were called *turpentine*) were used as astringents, placed on bleeding cuts or wounds, and left for several days after bandaging. The bitter roots and beans of a green marsh plant (*Menyanthes trifoliata*) called bog bean (or buck bean, or duck plant [Herbe au canard] bean [Peter Scott 31 July 1992, personal communication]) were used for the flu or to increase the appetite of those suffering from cancer. Settlers regularly consumed cod liver oil to prevent tuberculosis.

Settlers made lozenges from molasses and kerosene. One spoonful of kerosene was added to about two cups of molasses, heated to the soft boil stage, kneaded, and cut into small squares. Lozenges treated sore throats as did another treatment, a mixture of Friar's Balsam (tincture of benzene) and sugar.

Gatherings, puss-filled boils, were customarily treated with poultices. Bread poultices were most common: soft bread, excluding the crust, was boiled in water, placed over the gathering and bandaged. An older woman recalled once applying such a poultice to her husband just before the unexpected arrival of the Grenfell ship. The doctor aboard said that the poultice was as good as any treatment he might have provided. Less commonly, a poultice was made from a small bird, such as a sparrow. The bird was split open, and while still warm, placed on the gathering in order to bring it to a head. Another kind of poultice was used for chest colds. A mixture of kerosene, butter, and Miner's Liniment was heated on the stove and then rubbed on the patient's chest, which was then covered with a warm flannel cloth. This remedy was also applied to loosen a chest that had "tighten[ed] up," that is, the person was not able to cough up phlegm.

Fall Economic Activities

The amount of time spent at Cape Charles and other Labrador summer stations has steadily decreased in recent decades, primarily because of state intrusions such as the legislated school year. This annoys fishers, who claim September can be the best fishing month. Before the arrival of Earle Brothers at Battle Harbour in 1955, families used the months of September and October to *make* (i.e., sun dry) codfish. In 1979, most fishers had shipped their salt bulk fish and moved back to Lodge Bay by mid-September, so their children could resume school (persons without school-age children may remain at outside fishing stations for a few more weeks). The main reason that people once remained at outside fishing stations was to net harp seals and hunt migratory waterfowl. These once-vital fall economic activities are now only a memory for older residents. The decline of these activities and what older people believe is the premature move back to Lodge Bay means that autumn, especially prior to snow cover, is an economically ambiguous season.

New activities, both social and economic, have filled the gap. One of these is federally funded "make work" projects. For example, in recent years the Local Improvement Committee has obtained several grants to improve the rough gravel roads either at Lodge Bay or Cape Charles. When no codfish appeared after the 1977 salmon fishery, ten fishers left Cape Charles and returned to Lodge

Komatik, beaver, chainsaw, and small stumpbox. Lodge Bay.

Bay, where they built the present school. Some people (especially older couples and single individuals) also use the early fall for trips elsewhere in Labrador or, more commonly, to Corner Brook, Conception Bay, or St. John's, Newfoundland. Early fall is also a time for household repairs.

By October some hunting for partridge and migratory waterfowl takes place. Men set snares for rabbits, an important source of winter food, and also set traps for beaver, lynx, marten, fox, and other fur-bearing animals. While the extent of contemporary trapping should not be exaggerated, a few men enjoy trapping and some vestiges of trapping territories survive. Such territories were once regulated by the principle of the harbour rule; that is, they were locally devised and commonly agreed upon. Older male informants recall that one person trapped here, another person there, and that all a respected person's rights to animals on his trapping grounds. As one informant put it, "today nobody is really trapping"; yet some association with former trappers and their grounds persists. These vestiges of territoriality may be exemplified by the case of a man who moved to Lodge Bay from another Labrador community a couple of decades ago and who told me he no longer sets traps near Lodge Bay because he might be on another's grounds. The implication of his comment was that he had once done so and had probably been reprimanded. Those who trap mail their furs to the Hudson's Bay Company in St. John's or Blanc Sablon, Quebec, or to a buyer in Antigonish, Nova Scotia.

One of Lodge Bay's most active trappers reported the following catch during fall and winter 1978–79. In fall, he snared more than 300 rabbits, his biggest autumn catch ever. Along with his occasional trapping partner, he caught six beavers, using the common method of trapping beavers in their lodges. He also caught one *cross* and one red fox, fifteen to twenty muskrats, and a "nice few" weasels. He sold these furs to a buyer in Antigonish. This man's trapping effort and catch were above average but provide some idea of what now constitutes a good trapping season. I add that the high price of lynx in the late 1970s prompted much effort to trap them. The trapper just mentioned trapped no lynx in 1978–79 but trapped six during the winter of 1976–77.

Winter Economic Activities

By November snow covers the land. Soon bodies of freshwater freeze and some weeks later, saltwater bays freeze. By November snowmobiles replace foot travel and woods work begins. Older residents are quick to point out that contemporary woods work, with its snowmobiles and chainsaws, is only "fun" compared to the days when men used axes and cut between 1,000 and 1,500 *sticks* (logs) per winter.

Lodge Bay people use two kinds of sledges to haul wood. The *woodslide* is essentially a heavy sliding frame used for hauling sticks 3.5 to 4.5 meters long. The woodslide or slide (similar to what was once called a catamaran) is over 3 meters long and more than 60 centimeters wide. The vertical bars, attached to the runners, feature *wood horns* near the outside edge, and these contain the logs being towed. Just as the runners and vertical bars of the woodslide are proportionally stronger than those of the all-purpose komatik, so the metal brace and tow bars that permit the slide to be towed are more robust and bulky.

Locals use the all-purpose komatik to haul a variety of materials and/or people. If the woodslide is Labrador's semitrailer truck, then the komatik is its pickup. Komatik runners measure about 2.75 meters long and are shod with heavy metal strips; the front of each runner is curved up and often made of a separate piece joined to the straight runner. Nailed side by side to the runners, the bars form a continuous platform atop the runners. Typically, komatik bars measure about sixty centimeters long by about ten to fifteen centimeters wide and 2.5 centimeters thick. Today, komatik bars are nailed to the runners, providing less flexibility than the older method of lashing them. A nylon rope is attached by half hitches to the top outside edge of the komatik bars, enabling a *stumpbox* or *coachbox* to be tied atop the komatik. The stumpbox is made of relatively light yet strong plywood nailed to four corner posts that often have a curved horn protruding above the box. The woodslide and komatik are essential productive technologies; all households have at least one komatik, though the more specialized woodslides are somewhat less common.

Cutting and hauling firewood and sawing logs used for construction continues throughout the winter. Locals cut all their wood on Crown Land (government owned), which they view as common lands open to all on a first-come, first-served basis. The forests surrounding Lodge Bay extend about fifty kilometers west of the community; one then encounters the barrens, and still further inland, the main woods. The expanse of the forest and the notion that it belongs to all, mean that controversies surrounding individual rights to harvesting are rare.

People often travel fifteen to twenty kilometers to obtain good dry wood for fuel. Dry firewood is standing dead spruce or balsam fir trees, which have lost much of their moisture and sap content. Near

Winter. Lodge Bay man wearing a *cossack* checking his summer house at Cape Charles.

Lodge Bay many such trees have been cut out. Wood charred by forest fires (but not totally burned), locally called *blacky-boy timber*, is also prized (though messy to handle) as firewood. Dry larch (*Larix laricina*, locally called juniper) is often found in large marshes or bogs (locally called *meshes*).

Snowmobiles have reduced the burden (though not the cost) of obtaining firewood, and men sometimes cruise through an area where they believe dry wood will be found. Once, I accompanied the man of the first family I lived with, traveling twenty kilometers south of Lodge Bay before finding a stand of dry juniper on a windswept and snow-covered bog. He used his chainsaw to cut enough for a coachbox full of wood, all portioned into *junks* (pieces) of stove length. He had never been to this location before, nor did he know a place-name for it. But neither was he lost; he had cruised to the place and knew its approximate location in relationship to other known places.

Men enjoy such trips to the woods and make several each week, depending on their needs and on weather conditions. Wooding is hard (and dangerous) work, but it also offers time to think and to survey for forest and animal resources, and is perhaps also a temporary respite from the social constraints of life in a small community. Meanwhile, women remain at home with household work and young children. Many women find release in daily television soap operas.

Woods work continues until spring. In addition to firewood, most men cut some larger sawlogs for milling and use in boat, house, and wharf construction. Those planning on building boats in spring look for trees with large curved sections for use in making the *stems* of boats and for live juniper trees used in making steamed *crooked timbers* (essentially the ribs) of speedboats.

Spring Economic Activities

By mid-March, most men have completed their wood cutting, except for the hauling of a small load for burning or a few logs for sawing. Attention now shifts to the sawmilling of lumber and then to various building projects. In 1979 there were five individually owned and operated sawmills among the 125 people of Lodge Bay, perhaps the highest per capita number of sawmills in Canada! All five Lodge Bay mills were located in or near the community. Previously, sawmills had been disassembled and moved closer to the area where cutting was done to reduce the hauling of round sticks. The oldest of the five sawmill engines is a five horsepower Acadian made in Bridgewater, Nova Scotia. Three of the 1979 mills consisted of parts from one sawmill once jointly owned by three unrelated middle-aged men. Several years before the field period, the three divided the mill's machinery and acquired new machinery once their sons became young men, thus creating the basis for three separate mills.

Sawmills produce rough spruce boards, planks, posts, and so on. Those not owning a sawmill usually cut wood *on the halves*, that is, on shares; they deliver round sticks at a mill but receive only half of it back as lumber, with the mill owner taking the remaining half as payment. A skilled young boatbuilder, who owns Lodge Bay's only planer (and welding torch), planes rough lumber into finished lumber. He planes or welds at the rate of a few dollars per item.

Boats are important to southeastern Labrador people and people hold strong opinions about the recent history of boat-building. Port Hope Simpson people told me that in the old days, presumably in the 1930s and 1940s, few boats were built because knowledge of boat-building was limited to older people and not shared. In those days, an old man said, if you came upon a man building a boat and stopped to observe, he would stop working. Port Hope Simpson people added that cooperation and the sharing of knowledge is now more widespread, as is boat-building. Some thirty boats (trapboats and speedboats) were built in Port Hope Simpson in the spring of 1978.

Similar interpretations about the history of boat-building exist in St. Lewis (Fox Harbour) and Lodge Bay, though without the emphasis Port Hope Simpson people appear to place on sharing knowledge. Boat-building styles vary between communities. Fox Harbour speedboats, much admired by Lodge Bay boatbuilders, are distinguished by the fact that their interior timbers (essentially, the ribbing to which planks are nailed) are all bent timbers rather than a combination of steamed timbers and crocked knees used by Lodge Bay men. Speedboats from Battle Harbour and especially from nearby Indian Cove are described as having *raken' stems*, meaning that the angle of their keel and stem is considerably greater than that of Lodge Bay boats. The gunwales of Snug Harbour motorboats appear closer to the water line (unloaded) than do others along the coast; some Snug Harbour boats are equipped with a *sculling hole*, and I observed the ancient sculling oar in use there. Finally, Sandwich Bay was once known for *lapstrake* boat construction, that is, for boats in which each of the exterior planks overlapped that below it, somewhat like clapboard on an exterior house wall.

Though no account can be given here, it is probable that each boat style illustrates both the diffusion of boat-building techniques from elsewhere, perhaps a measure of expressive difference, and the adaptation of these methods to local ocean conditions. Thus,

Rodney on komatik. Lodge Bay.

the heavy boats built at Lodge Bay are suited to the rough water conditions at Cape Charles.

In the spring of 1979, one motorboat, seven speedboats, one punt, one flat, and one dory were built at Lodge Bay. (The punt, flat, and dory are all small wooden rowboats.) One young Lodge Bay boatbuilder constructed a large, Cape Island–style boat during the previous winter and spring. This was the most ambitious boat-building project in recent years.

The amount of time consumed building a boat varies with the builder's experience, the availability of lumber, and the type of boat constructed. Five- to six-meter-long speedboats can be built in about two weeks. During spring 1979, I spent about that amount of time watching and occasionally helping a man build a speedboat. Smaller boats, such as punts, can be built in less time; one man built a punt with *solid knees* in three days.

Around early May, the ice in the St. Charles River begins to break up. The insecurity of river ice makes the safety of skidoo travel across the river a topic of daily conversations. Some school days are inevitably missed, and many phone conversations take place between households on both sides of the river, arranging for schoolchildren to be picked up or dropped off by boat. By this time of year people's thoughts increasingly turn to the open water season ahead, and boat building or boat painting continues in earnest. A variety of tasks ultimately related to the open water season consumes people's energies. For example, a man needing new *paddles* (oars) for a speed- or motorboat may take advantage of a rainy day to make them. People use *vir* (balsam fir), and occasionally spruce wood to make paddles. Motorboat paddles are about four meters long and may be roughed out first with an ax and later planed with an electric plane, a hand plane, or a spoke shave.

Once open water permits, people launch motor- and speedboats from their winter resting places on slipways. Some may haul loads of firewood in motorboats to Cape Charles. This method of boating wood (or hauling it by snowmobile in winter) is the modern equivalent of the rafting of wood that once took place. In contrast, historic rafting of wood involved placing many logs beside one another, resembling ribs on corduroy cloth. The next layer of ribbed logs ran in a perpendicular direction from those of the first raft; several more layers were placed atop the others. The whole tiered assembly was either put together at Raft Island (between Lodge Bay and Cape Charles) or towed there, and from there towed to Cape Charles.

Spring launching of a motorboat at Lodge Bay. Note slipway.

By early spring local shops are occasionally short of supplies, especially fresh meat and produce. Most of the dry goods and produce in Lodge Bay's three small shops is shipped by coastal boat in late fall, but in recent years these stocks, especially fresh produce, are supplemented throughout the winter by shipments carried on chartered planes. By May unpredictable river ice prevents planes from landing near the community. Shop owners buy their stock on credit and pay interest (in 1979, 1.5 percent per month) on goods not sold. This often makes it more profitable to pay the high air charter fees and import popular and quick-selling items like fresh meat, ice cream, fruit, and confectioneries than to stockpile enough of these goods to last all winter.

When open water permits, locals supplement their diet with fresh trout, mussels, and clams. Some people set trout nets along the river bisecting the community, even though informants claimed that they catch few trout or salmon descending the St. Charles river in spring. Alternatively, people set their nets several kilometers outside the community, and these perhaps catch sea trout endemic to tributaries of the St. Charles River. Some people claimed that it is possible to net salmon and trout near Lodge Bay in August and September while others said overfishing in 1970 destroyed the river's fish population. Locals gather saltwater clams in mud flats near the community and collect mussels throughout the open water season near Cape Charles and other sites on the outer coast.

The Cash Economy

In addition to the seasonal extraction of local natural resources, cash enters most Lodge Bay households through various federal transfer payments and job creation programs. Southard (1981; 1982) deals with the cash economy of nearby Port Hope Simpson in considerable detail, and therefore I provide only a brief description here.

Unemployed people who accumulated a sufficient number of insurable weeks of employment prior to ending work are eligible for federal Unemployment Insurance benefits. Introduced in 1940 to sustain Canadians temporarily out of work or between jobs, the UI program was amended in 1957 to insure self-employed fishers. Like their counterparts in the shop or factory, self-employed fishers must accumulate a minimum (though ever increasing) number of insurable weeks (eight in 1979), and do so through sales of fish to a buyer, who, for purposes of the UI Act, is deemed the fisher's or plant worker's employer. Fishers accumulating a minimum number of insurable weeks (or stamps) earned from fishing or from additional work, then report their earnings, that is, actual sales of fish, less expenses. Seasonal UI benefits are ordinarily drawn between 1 November and 15 May. Benefits may be up to 60 percent of the average net earnings from fishing, meaning that the more a fisher (or wage worker) earns, the higher his/her weekly UI payments will be. Unemployment Insurance earnings are an extremely important source of cash income in all economically marginal areas of Canada; Lodge Bay is no exception. Seasonal reliance on UI payments carries no local stigma and rural people throughout Atlantic Canada clearly distinguish between UI and social assistance. Whereas UI is considered a right, social assistance can tarnish one's standing in the community. Critics of the immense role of UI in rural economies like that of Lodge Bay claim with some justification that the UI system has diverged from its original purpose and now functions as an income supplement to economically marginal Canadians (Newfoundland 1986).

The provincial government provides social assistance to individuals or families unable to work because of illness or to people whose UI payments have expired and have been unable to find new work. The duration of social assistance is either long term, in the case of debilitating diseases preventing people from working or, more commonly, short-term relief. Short-term relief payments vary by season, with spring and then fall being the periods of greatest need. Table 2 presents statistics for the number of individuals on long- and short-term social assistance in communities near Lodge Bay in 1979. As can be seen, certain communities, notably Cape Charles and Williams Harbour, rely less on social assistance than do others in the area, such as Port Hope Simpson and St. Lewis.

Federal transfer payments include monies provided to all Canadians over age 65 (Old Age Security). In 1979, five persons in Lodge Bay (4.8 percent) obtained Old Age Security payments. Transfer payments also include a family allowance. Federal family allowance payments are made monthly to all unmarried children less than 21 years old living with their parents. The amount of these payments are categorized according to age, with younger children receiving less than older ones.

Like many rural Canadian communities, Lodge Bay normally receives a Canada Works project, providing short-term (a minimum of thirteen weeks) local employment, usually during winter or spring. In Lodge Bay the elected three-member Local Improvement Committee recommends potential winter works projects to the East Shore Labrador Development Association, a regional development organization representing communities in the southern half of the

Table 2   SOCIAL ASSISTANCE

Community	Quarter Ending				
	31 Sept 1978	31 Dec 1978	31 Mar 1979	21 June 1979	Long-term
Port Hope Simpson	29	47	29	64	8
Pinsent's Arm	—	2	3	4	—
Cape Charles	—	—	1	—	7
Mary's Harbour	10	19	6	10	7
William's Harbour	—	—	—	5	—
St. Lewis (Fox. Hr)	3	5	6	8	9
Square Islands	5	11	7	15	3
Snug Harbour	6	6	6	6	—

Source: Social Assistance Office, Mary's Harbour, 1979.

region, between Lodge Bay and Snug Harbour. The Development Association then ranks projects from the communities it represents and forwards its recommendations to the provincial Department of Rural Development. In the spring of 1979, the Canada Works Project at Lodge Bay extended the existing herring facility at Cape Charles; a one-story extension was added, measuring about six by nine meters and set on pilings.

Canada Works projects frequently cause problems in the communities that receive them. It must be understood that the 1979 project involved an approximately nineteen-kilometer journey from

Cape Charles in winter. Herring facility is white building in center of photo. Frozen sea ice surrounds.

Lodge Bay to the work site at Cape Charles. By the time work began in early April, snow and ice conditions for snowmobile travel were deteriorating, meaning increased wear and tear on expensive snowmobiles used to commute.

A Local Improvement Committee member, whom I shall call Peter, vigorously supported the project because, among other things, the Labrador Strait merchant who leased the facility needed more space to house herring-cutting tables that would permit increased secondary herring processing at Cape Charles. Peter believed the extended facility would create additional work during summer. Peter has a long-standing and sincere involvement with community work; he is secretary-treasurer of the Local Improvement Committee and has frequently represented Lodge Bay at regional conferences. While in hindsight Peter might be criticized for his dogged loyalty to the project despite the deteriorating snow and ice conditions, his motives were altruistic. His main objective was for the development of the community.

As events unfolded, Peter was attending a development meeting in another Labrador community in late March and phoned home to inquire how things were going in Lodge Bay. He was bitterly disappointed to learn that very few men were willing to risk ruining their snowmobiles to work on the project. He was so distraught by this news that he broke down at the meetings in front of other community representatives.

Days later, when Peter returned to Lodge Bay, enthusiasm for the project remained low. However, given that the project provided locally available work, men eventually "volunteered" when faced with the threat from Canada Manpower that anyone unwilling to work might not receive UI benefits. Peter served as project foreman, and his crew included a dozen or so single young men. Most families who were able to contribute a son did so, apparently because of an unspoken understanding to spread the burden of the project throughout the community. The daily commute took more than two hours, leading some workers to stay overnight at Cape Charles. However, most people believed that the low weekly wages ($125), the travel stipend of $30 per man per week, the automatic loss of UI payments while working, and the long and rough snowmobile trip to and from the work site produced few economic benefits. The project was completed by early summer, but its political repercussions lingered for some time.

Many Lodge Bay people believed that those who successfully avoided working on the unpopular 1979 Canada Works project were hoping that if one was awarded for 1980, it would be located nearer Lodge Bay and thus cause less damage to snowmobiles. Those men who avoided work on the 1979 project were generally older, family men. Many were busy building boats, and Canada Manpower apparently interpreted this as a deferment from having to work on the project. Consequently, they continued to receive UI. Peter complained to me that one of Lodge Bay's most skilled boatbuilders had used the boat-building "excuse" to avoid working on the 1978 and 1979 projects.

By way of comparison, Canada Works Projects resemble Great Britain's Job Creation Programmes, as described by F. MacKay, M. P. Jackson, and V. J. B. Hanley (1980) in relation to West Scottish crofting communities. Like marginal regions of Canada, the approximately 30,000 people of the Western Isles have a fragile mixed economy, a history of high unemployment, and periodic out-migration. National Job Creation programmes have cut unemployment, reduced out-migration, and enhanced community facilities. The programs are also valued because they have enabled the youth to become integrated into the community. However, MacKay, Jackson, and Hanley (1980) conclude on an ominous note very relevant to Labrador: national work creation schemes are as vulnerable as the regions they serve, and they are subject to political change, potentially leaving in the lurch people dependent on them. When such programs are withdrawn or reduced, marginal regions suffer.

Chapter 4

Social and Political Life

Social History and Archaic Settlement

Lodge Bay Settlers are keenly interested in their history. The two questions they most often ask are identical to those asked by the Spanish peasants described by Ruth Behar: "how did their community come into existence and who were its first settlers?" (1991, 269). Unfortunately, in the case of Lodge Bay, the answers to these questions may never be known. However, drawing on field notes, the 1935 nominal census, and from the Battle Harbour church records, one gets a general overview of social history and archaic settlement.

The vast majority of Lodge Bay's 1979 population may be traced to one of three maximal male ancestors, of which two (Moses and James Pye) were definitely brothers. (It is possible that all three were brothers, and children of the "W. Pye" mentioned in the 1832 "Moss Diary" at Battle Harbour.) The most influential of these "lineages" derives from James Pye (1830–93). It is also the largest, because James and his wife produced at least nine children, and many of these remained in the community. Five of these nine were brothers and of these, four produced children who are the fathers or grandfathers of many of today's population. One of the five sons, Ephrain (remembered as Uncle Eef), is especially interesting in that only one of his five children was a male. This son entered the armed services during World War I and settled permanently in Corner Brook, Newfoundland, after the war. Lacking male heirs in Lodge Bay, Ephrain and his wife adopted a Newfoundland boy, Thomas

James (born 1892). At about age 23, Thomas James married and he and his wife had five boys and four girls. Significantly all five sons remained in Lodge Bay and produced average- to large-size families. Consequently, as some biological Pyes now point out, over one-third of Lodge Bay's population may be traced to the adopted Thomas James Pye.

James's brother Moses (1846–1926), the second maximal ancestor, and his wife had seven boys and three girls but only two of the boys, James M. and William are important kin links to the contemporary population.

The third apparent maximal male ancestor to the contemporary population is Edmund Pye (1835–1907). He and his wife had three boys and six girls but only two of these children, Lorenzo and Susan, are important progenitors to the present population. Lorenzo and his wife had ten children but most of them remained single. Only one son, Alfred, produced offspring that are counted in today's population. Susan married John Pye and had a son, Leslie. Leslie and his wife had no children and consequently adopted a nine-year-old Corner Brook boy, whom we shall call Walt Smith. Walt remained in the community, married, and had children.

Historically, female out-migration has been endemic to Newfoundland and Labrador fishing communities. Some traveled to Newfoundland to work as domestics or, more recently, to work in other capacities. A few traveled to Canada or to the United States. Of course not all women who left Lodge Bay left Labrador. Many married men from Henley Harbour, Battle Harbour, or other nearby communities. Others traveled to Newfoundland to work as domestics or, more recently, to work in other capacities. A few traveled to Canada or to the United States.

During the late nineteenth and early twentieth century two winter settlements existed on the periphery of present day Lodge Bay. The historic Rabbit Brook settlement was located on the eastern end of contemporary Lodge Bay, and another old settlement, which I will call the River settlement, was located three kilometers west. Before the fire of August 1946, many of the ancestors of the present population, particularly of the Lorenzo and Thomas James Pye lineages, lived at Rabbit Brook. Also living at Rabbit Brook were families such as Bellows, Riggs, Buckingham, and Griffin, surnames no longer found in Lodge Bay.

The River settlement, containing two neighborhoods, was located about three kilometers west of Rabbit Brook, primarily along the wooded banks of the north side of St. Charles River, or as residents say, "up the river" or "up the brook." Informants claim that people settled "up the river" to "hide away" or "avoid

Men at work in Lodge Bay, c. 1935. Older man holding hand plane. Note black sheep in foreground. (Photograph courtesy of Verna Pye)

warships," a very common folk theory of early settlement in New-foundland and Labrador. Noteworthy is the fact that this older settlement lacked sufficient water depths to allow access by boat. Contemporary informants speak respectfully of the *old people* carrying kitchen stoves and other possessions on their backs during seasonal moves to and from Cape Charles or another outside fishing station. Unlike in modern Lodge Bay, the majority of homes "up the river" were situated on the north side of the river, possibly because its orientation provided more sunlight and therefore was warmer.

In May 1979, two older male informants guided my foot survey of the River settlement. Two neighborhoods—the Rapids and Kennelly's Brook—form this settlement.* The older Rapids neigh-borhood once contained at least five homes and a school. (People said there was once a school for Rabbit Brook and one up the river;

---

* The name (or names) Kennelly has several spellings (e.g., Kenneally or Kennenally) and appears to have a distant and largely forgotten relationship with Lodge Bay and Cape Charles. The name does not occur in the Battle Harbour Anglican church records but may be associated with Carbonear Kenneallys, including John Kennenally.

Leslie and Fanny Pye, c. 1940. (Photograph courtesy of Verna Pye)

teachers alternated periodically until controversy led to an amalgamated school, built near the present school, in about 1927). The Rapids homes include those of three sons and a daughter of James Pye and Mary Ann Soper, all born between 1858 and 1866. This suggests that the homes could have been occupied as early as the 1880s. The sister, Mary Ann, married Elijah Horwood. I cannot explain why the other home, which belonged to Henry and Julia Hunt, was located in this neighborhood, but I suspect that Julia was a Pye, perhaps Julia Mary (born 1875 of Edmund and Julia). The Hunts later wintered at Cowhouse (south of Lodge Bay) and moved to Corner Brook, Newfoundland, after their two sons drowned, in 1927.

A couple of hundred meters downstream, Kennelly's Brook empties into the St. Charles River. Here one encounters the barely visible foundations and meager debris of the second, and more recent, historic neighborhood. Henry Thomas, the youngest son of James Pye and Mary Ann Soper, had a house here. Also the three sons of James V. Pye, all born between 1905 and 1913, had houses here, as did Ken Pye, John Pye and others—a total of about ten houses. This neighborhood was occupied during the first half of this century, until the forest fire of August 1946.

Contemporary Lodge Bay Neighborhoods

Given the historic pattern of brothers living so near each other, we should hardly be surprised to see a similar pattern in contemporary Lodge Bay. Indeed, most close kin, particularly brothers, live as neighbors in kin-based enclaves nestled along both sides of the St. Charles River. Most of these adult sons have built homes along the spacious north side of the river, across from their parents' homes. Brothers Samson, Jim, and Tom, and neighbor Herb live on the north side of the river, just across from their parents. Also on the north side is Lester, just opposite his older brother and widowed mother. The other main enclave of four brothers and two sisters, offspring of the adopted Thomas James Pye, extends along most of the south side of the river.

The Life Cycle

The term life cycle refers to a series of status changes individuals pass through, beginning with birth and ending with death. In 1979 a Grenfell mission policy stipulated that pregnant women must deliver at nearby Mary's Harbour clinic or the hospital in St. Anthony. Newborns are lavished with attention, and by the time they become toddlers, they rule the roost, remaining awake and active late into the night, crying when their demands (often materialistic) are not met and generally vying for the attention of their parents.

Young children are treated with considerable leniency. On one occasion, I observed a seven-year-old boy cry periodically for a day or so for a new school bag he had seen in a local shop. Once his parents gave in and purchased the bag, it turned out to be poorly constructed and lasted only two weeks. Children are permitted to play with just about everything. I once observed a father repairing one of his two chainsaws, in preparation for cutting firewood. He performed the task in the front entryway of the house where the family's two-year-old son proceeded to pick, pull, drop, and handle the saw parts as soon as his father dismantled them. The only discouragement the child received was familiar warnings such as "What are you doing?" or "Get out of *that!*" Despite this extra work, the father successfully completed the repairs.

Lodge Bay birthday party.

Children receive little corporal punishment except for an infrequent threat of or gentle slap on the hand. More frequently, they are told with an almost pleaful scolding to "be good" or in more extreme instances warned, "You better not get into *that*, buddy." Mothers devote most of their waking hours to children, particularly when there are several, each of which may take turns in what amounts to a continuous filibuster for parental attention. For their part, parents lament that their children are "spoiled," and older Lodge Bay people say that today's children are "given too much" and "made too much of." They contrast the present with the past, when parents gave their children more responsibilities around the house. Instead of physical punishment, parents have always used supernatural and threatening characters to encourage proper behavior.

Grandfather pulls grandchildren and plastic water pails. Rabbit Brook, Lodge Bay.

Youth Peer Groups

As the community population pyramid of 1979 shows, males and females are especially numerous in the 6 to 10 and 11 to 15 age cohorts, and it is common to see boys and girls in both age cohorts in sexually separate groups playing or walking along the road. Children often play at *copying*, that is, at imitating adult behavior. At Cape Charles and other fishing settlements, young boys may tie a few meters of old fish net to boulders along the beach during low tide and the next day empty it of the sculpins and flat fish it has caught. I once passed several boys aged 7 to 11 who were playing with a short portion of old net and asked *how* they were doing. Characteristically, my query prompted a description of *what* they were doing—in their case, "getting our gear ready, by." Similarly, young girls copy at playing house by converting part of an old cardboard box into a house.

Of course boundaries between the age cohorts in the population pyramid are arbitrary and artificially fixed; boundaries between age statuses in real life are more variable and are defined by changes in physical development. The onset of puberty between age 10 to 13 propels children into adolescence. There are additional means by which this transformation may be signaled. I once overheard a conversation between a mother and her three young children about the necessity that they have their hair cut. Until then, all, including the eldest, nine-year-old Mary, had had their hair cut by their grandparents. But now when Mary asked if her grandparents would also cut *her* hair, her mother told her that she should ask Jean, a young Lodge Bay wife who cuts the hair of many of the community's adolescent and adult women.

Boundaries between youth peer groups are continuously tested and maintained. Early one August 1980 evening at Cape Charles, I observed three adolescent boys (aged 14 to 17) sauntering along the community's winding gravel road. All helped their fathers with the fishery during the day, but now they were out on the town, dressed in the popular attire of leather motorcycle-styled jackets, blue jeans, and low black rubber boots. But several younger boys walked only a couple of meters behind the youths, mimicking and taunting the older three. Every so often the derision of the younger group caused their three older victims to angrily turn around, scattering their annoying juniors.

In the evening, after their household chores are completed, small groups of adolescent girls can be seen walking through the community. Sometimes the girls walk arm in arm, and occasionally a giggle may be heard. Most of these girls will eventually leave the community. Whereas the fishery may employ their brothers, it offers few opportunities for women. By the time they reach age 11 to 15, their thoughts turn to the world beyond their community. Television, radio, and other intrusions attract their attention.

Single Men's Peer Group

In addition to the adolescent male peer group mentioned above, there is another male peer group composed of most of the community's single men of marriageable age. In 1979, the core of this

Girls rowing rodney with motorboat in background. Cape Charles.

group numbered eight men between the ages of 18 and 29. Most of this group congregate during winter nights at the home of Ike, the 32-year-old married father of the family where I boarded. Younger males in their mid-teens sometimes arrive at Ike's house before the older male peer group. The arrival of the senior group soon quiets their more boisterous juniors, who may also retreat to the less populated periphery of the room and listen.

The older single young men spend such evenings sitting around Ike's kitchen table, talking about snowmobiles (usually the merits of their own, but sometimes more generally), whatever significant happened to them that day, or current gossip. Conversations about national news or sports, such as hockey, are rare, as young Lodge Bay men have little interest in sports. A favorite and competitive way of passing the time is arguing over rival interpretations of minutiae.

Young men occasionally play cards or darts at Ike's house. They often consume beer, although most nights few become intoxicated. If beer runs out, one or more of the men collect money and travel by snowmobile to Mary's Harbour for more. Other nights, typically late, a collection may be taken up to buy a *lunch* of frozen chicken and chips, heated in Ike's oven.

The young men enjoy joking and roughhousing. During the field period a rather acquiescent young male school teacher from Newfoundland befriended men of the single male group. The youths liked the young teacher who was unable or unwilling to defend himself physically against their interminable pranks. Consequently, several times he was the victim of one of their favorite jests—having his pants pulled off.

Two points especially surprised me about the single adult male group. First was their apparent sexual inactivity. In fairness, there were few available females in Lodge Bay aged 16 to 25. Nor were there rumors about any sexual affairs between the young men and local married women. There are more women in nearby Mary's Harbour, and some from the single male group claimed to have girlfriends there or in other communities. But generally talk about women and evidence of sexual involvement seemed dwarfed by other interests. And finally, homosexuality appears rare or absent.

The second point that surprised me about the young men's peer group was its solidarity, particularly given that they are together daily much of the year. Relative harmony is also remarkable, given that the eight most constant members of the group come from five different families that in a sense compete for scarce resources much of the year. Even when fistfights occur between the young men, they do not appear to hinder the long-term cohesiveness of the group. One such fight occurred on 16 April 1979 between Hector and Dick. At the time, both were employed on the unpopular Canada Works project at Cape Charles. The next day Hector avoided eating with the others at the Cape and did not visit Ike's that night. The others interpreted this as meaning he had wrongly instigated the fight or was embarrassed for other reasons. But such fights are rare and do not produce lasting fissures in group togetherness.

Sex and Marriage

Like many aspects of contemporary Lodge Bay life, attitudes concerning sexual behavior are continuously changing. The access to modern methods of birth control at the Mary's Harbour Grenfell clinic, plus intrusive influences ranging from new people to television mean that sex is becoming a form of recreation as much as of procreation. Some evidence for changing sexual behavior comes from incidents I observed involving social interaction between local men and those who either came from or had traveled outside Labrador. For example, I once observed a conversation between a Lodge Bay man, Bill, who has lived and traveled extensively throughout Canada; another man, Pete, from a Labrador Straits community; and Bob, a less-traveled 16-year-old local youth. While splitting fish at a Cape Charles stage, Bill and Pete jokingly asked Bob if he had ever "eaten at the Y." A nervous and confused Bob struggled with the queries. They probably referred to the sexual practice of cunnilingus, which a local informant claimed had diffused to the area only a few years previously.

Most people in southeast Labrador have a naturalistic attitude toward sex. When speaking about the fact that young people of one community have lovers in another, one woman (not from Lodge Bay) used a metaphor from the maintenance of fishing gear to explain the sexual drive of her community's youth. "You gotta bit of gear, you gotta tend it."

The region's long-standing pattern of female out-migration always led to a shortage of women. An older Lodge Bay bachelor claimed that "if you wanted to have a little foolin' round, you had to go out o' it." He went on to explain that female out-migration "drove a lot of fellows out of it. It's only so long without a woman or something like that, you go somewhere." This bachelor claimed to still "fool around," particularly when he traveled to Newfoundland, where he claimed women were a "dime a dozen."

Four of the Lodge Bay's twenty men aged 36 to 70 (or 20 percent) are bachelors. However, bachelors readily acknowledge the importance of women. As one put it, "That's part of life, you gotta have women." Given the lack of eligible women in Lodge Bay, prohibitions against marrying too close, and the necessity of men remaining with the fishery, it is probable that some in the young men's peer group will never marry. Indeed, the bachelor status is common to the whole region; yet few people agree on why men (and to a lesser extent, women) remain single. My direct question to one Lodge Bay bachelor on this produced this response: "Now when I was younger . . . I used to like girls . . . foolin' around, but gettin' married, when I thought about it, and really, I never seen anybody I wanted . . . not that bad. And perhaps the ones I wanted I couldn't get."

In a society where marriage and having children are considered "natural" and highly valued, bachelors are viewed with a mixture of humor and pity. Bachelors are more socially marginal than married men. Most exhibit tendencies toward hypochondria and reclusion. One of the four is probably a paranoid schizophrenic who suffers from what is locally called "nerves," that is, an anxious and occasionally depressed state preventing him from carrying out routine daily activities (Davis 1983). Another bachelor claims to suffer from a variety of ailments, ranging from chronic ear infections to heart problems, while another of the four has an exceedingly cynical and bitter perspective on life. I lack sufficient life history data to state whether any of these characteristics led to bachelorhood, or vice versa.

Bachelors tend to be materially "poor." Medical reasons prevent two of the four from working. Single-occupant bachelor homes are more humble and sparsely furnished than those of most married men. In one two-story bachelor house, there is an old Ensign brand wood cooking/heating stove, a dilapidated couch in one corner under a stairway to a loft, a wash pan in another corner, cans of soup in the entry porch, and so on. Absent are the televisions, stereos, electric appliances, and other expensive possessions common to family homes.

Bachelors aside, most Lodge Bay men and women do marry. In over half of the marriages in the 1979 census, Lodge Bay men married women from other Labrador communities, notably Mary's Harbour, but also St. Lewis, Cartwright, and Red Bay, and from Newfoundland. These communities appear to have replaced Henley Harbour (and its winter settlement, Pitt's Arm), which closed in 1970, that had in the past often exchanged its sons and daughters with those from Lodge Bay as marriage partners.

Beginning in the 1970s, some Lodge Bay people married spouses from St. Lewis (Fox Harbour), where aboriginal physical characteristics are evident in some families. This led to the expression of veiled racial antipathy by some older Lodge Bay folk. When discussing changing marriage patterns, one Lodge Bay woman claimed young people were "going all out for them" (St. Lewis people). She added candidly that in her day (1920s and 1930s), Lodge Bay people "didn't know much about them Fox Harbour people, and, to be honest, we didn't care much about them."

Old Age and Death

As the population pyramid shows, in 1979 Lodge Bay had five men and one woman over the age of 66. (See chapter 6.) The woman comes from another southeastern Labrador community and is the single aunt of a Lodge Bay woman with whom she lives. Two of the five men are bachelors; one is from the abandoned community of Pitt's Arm and moved to Lodge Bay where he boards with his niece and her family. The other lives alone. The other three are married pensioners and live with their spouses. Of these, two have children living with them. Canada Old Age benefits begin automatically at age 65, helping older people maintain some economic independence, particularly when supplemented by the labors of older children living with or near them.

Older people are generally treated well by younger people. One of the few older people who occasionally endures some chiding from the young men is old Clint, one of the three bachelors who lives alone. In his case, however, the good-natured taunting (often about his presumably nonexistent sex life) and practical jokes he endures probably stem more from his petulant disposition and single status than from his age. Generally, however, the experience of older people is appreciated and there is little evidence of a generation gap. Older people do not attend the youth dances at the community hall, but they do dance with younger people at local house parties. That older people are accepted by younger people may be related to the community's fascination with history. As with all age groups within the region, older people who moved to Lodge Bay maintain strong emotional ties with the community where they were raised, always identifying it as "home" despite years of residence in Lodge Bay.

No one died during the field period, but in the spring of 1980 a 17-year-old Lodge Bay boy died suddenly of unknown causes. His untimely death shocked all and lingered like a morose pall during my summer 1980 visit.

Since the 1970s Lodge Bay residents have buried most of their dead in Lodge Bay's small and relatively new cemetery, which replaced the older and larger cemetery at Shoal Cove, Simm's Bay (south of Cape Charles), where at least fifty-four names are legible on headstones. This recent burial of dead at Lodge Bay rather than at Shoal Cove illustrates the decreasing use of outside fishing settlements. Both these cemeteries are Anglican, but it is important to note that historically there were also Catholic cemeteries, just as today there are Pentecostal cemeteries in other southeastern Labrador communities. Near Battle Harbour, for example, both Protestant and Catholic cemeteries may be found, the latter containing the remains of Catholics who once inhabited the area.

Voluntary Associations

In 1979 Lodge Bay people participated in several voluntary associations, including a Dart League, the Royal Orange Lodge, Anglican Church Women (ACW), and others. These organizations meet according to a regular weekly schedule between fall and spring and play an important role in the sociopolitical life of the community. In 1979, the Anglican Church Women met on Tuesday nights, the Dart League played at the community hall on

Easter Orangemen's parade at Lodge Bay.

Wednesday nights, Orange Lodge met on Friday nights, and the Junior Dart League (for children) on Saturdays. The Orange Lodge and the Anglican Church Women have a religious basis. Most of Lodge Bay's married men belong to the Orange Lodge. Orangemen from Red Bay brought the idea for an Orange Lodge to Lodge Bay about 1965. While the Orange Lodge members meet regularly at the community hall, their presence in the community is most obvious during the Easter parade around the community.

Local Orangemen made preparations for the 1979 Easter parade and the Easter night *time* at a meeting at the Orange Lodge two days prior to Easter. Twenty-seven Lodge members marched, including four from nearby Mary's Harbour. The marchers gathered at the community's Orange Lodge before marching first along the north side and then the south side of the river, to the school/church. There the second Anglican service of the day was held. Whereas the Easter morning service was attended primarily by women and children, the service following the march was heavily attended by men—they filled the first three rows. After the service, Orangemen marched again around part of the harbor, before marching back to the Orange Lodge. Before entering the Community Hall, several members raised their arms to form an arch before the door.

Orange Lodge members forming arch to enter hall after Easter parade.

Members entered the building one at time, filing on alternate sides of Peter Pye, who stood holding a box containing the Bible. To my surprise—and for the first time—I was invited inside. Members were first called to attention and officially ended the march by singing "God Save the Queen." Later that night, the Orangemen hosted a time at the community hall, which raised some $600.

Most of Lodge Bay's married women belong to the Anglican Church Women's group. The ACW organizes suppers and times at the hall. For example, in late February 1979, the ACW held a soup supper/dance to raise money to purchase new church books. Women brought *boilers* (large cauldrons) of salt beef, rabbit, or partridge soup, bread, and assorted desserts. Before the dancing began, the women auctioned woolen mittens, socks, and other locally crafted items. As is common at such times people from other communities, in this case, Mary's Harbour and St. Lewis, attended. The time raised between $500 and $600.

Fund-raising times are common throughout the region and are a remarkably persistent custom. For example, W. S. Abbott (1974) accompanied Lodge Bay folk to a Henley Harbour time during Easter 1963. The main difference between that time and those I participated in was the idiom of music and dance. The Henley Harbour time featured traditional accordion music and square dancing while Lodge Bay times featured live or recorded rock and roll music and modern dancing.

Political Organization

The politics of Lodge Bay may be discussed at several levels of ascending formality—the informal politics of gossip and argumentation, formal local politics, and regional and provincial politics. From time to time disputes erupt between families. Tensions occasionally explode into heated confrontations, but are more commonly vented through gossip or character denunciations, both occurring well out of range of the accused. One such dispute arose over the contamination of a local water supply. Bill is said to have accidentally contaminated the water supply used by several of his neighbors. Bill and his neighbor Bob got together and agreed to jointly dig a new well near the ruined one. One evening after the two had begun work, Bob rushed over to Bill's with the news that John, one of those who had used the allegedly ruined water supply, was digging a *brook* (well) just uphill from the well Bill and Bob had begun. Bill and Bob worried that John's new well would lessen their chances of obtaining water from their planned well. In his anger, Bob told Bill that he might call the Mountie (from the Royal Canadian Mounted Police) in Mary's Harbour to straighten things out. Bob did not, however, and instead broached the issue with John. Bill later told me how allegations about his accidental destruction of the water supply troubled him to the point that he considered moving across the river. He also claimed to have asked the chairman of the Local Improvement Committee for a public meeting to propose digging a community water supply but was told that the well he had ruined had always been good enough. Disputes like this may persist like open sores, with or without direct confrontations between disputants.

Bob's reputation might have suffered permanent damage had he taken his complaint to the Mounties. Indeed, there are rules governing conflict resolution. Overt hostility is scorned, and prestige is lost each time a person displays his/her temper. An example of loss of temper occurred in late May 1979 in events surrounding a common banquet for the Junior Dart and Floor Hockey Leagues. Mary arrived at the banquet without her expected donation, a boiler of soup. When Mary entered the hall, Ann, the organizer of the event, publicly reprimanded Mary for not bringing the soup. Mary responded that she had not been contacted, and she then angrily left the hall saying she would *never* again volunteer her time or money for a community event. She later told me, "I can't help it if she [Ann] has no shame . . . it's a horrible thing being *bawled out* in front of a crowd of adults." Mary later calmed down and two days later donated two cans of meat as prizes for a card game to benefit the Cape Charles school.

The Lodge Bay–Cape Charles area has an elected Local Improvement Committee, the type of municipal government the province recognizes in unincorporated communities. In 1979, the three-person committee included Gus, the chairman; Samson, the vice-chairman; and Peter, the secretary-treasurer. All are married men and are also active in regional politics. (Single men and women have little involvement in local politics.) Committee members serve four-year terms, and the committee is the main political connection between the community and the province. As noted, the committee also decides on applications for federal programs, such as the unpopular 1979 Canada Works project. We will recall that Peter, the project's most dedicated supporter, once publicly broke down upon learning of difficulties in recruiting labor for the project. On another occasion, this time in Lodge Bay, the newly formed recreation committee discussed problems with the 1979 project during a public meeting. Peter got up and walked out, followed by his wife.

Given that there are limits to which emotions can be expressed in most social interactions, it is surprising that verbal outbursts and sudden resignations are occasionally used as political tactics in public meetings. The apparent intent of such displays is to pressure those present to reconsider their position, so that harmony can be restored. Normally, however, community meetings are relaxed affairs. Leaders joke with others present, creating an air of nonchalance and the impression that little matters, even when the agenda contains serious issues. Public meetings seem to have both social and political functions.

Several Lodge Bay people participate in regional political organizations such as the Labrador Resource Advisory Council (LRAC), the Labrador Craft Producers Association, and the East Shore Labrador Development Association. However, people view provincial and federal politics with both uncertainty and cynicism. A few question whether southeastern Labrador should even be part of Newfoundland, and such separatist sentiments were expressed during the election of 1979. One man noted that the Liberal party campaign literature depicted Labrador as joined to Newfoundland at the Strait of Belle Isle. He remarked, "They make it look as if they're connected until just after the election." The man's brother declared that Labrador should be a territory separate from Newfoundland.

Since the provincial electoral redistribution of 1974, Lodge Bay has been part of the Eagle River political district. I was in Lodge Bay during the provincial election of June 1979. The Liberal party candidate was a Newfoundlander who visited Labrador for the first time during the campaign, reportedly carrying a school geography book with a map and description of the region. The Progressive Conservative party candidate was a native of Mary's Harbour who had traveled extensively throughout Labrador when doing regional political work with the LRAC and in his job as a fieldworker with Memorial University Extension. The New Democratic Party (NDP) party candidate was a woman from the Labrador Strait and was relatively unknown in the region.

The Liberal candidate visited Cape Charles late one Saturday night, arriving aboard a hired speedboat driven by a Mary's Harbour fisher. Most people had turned off their electrical generators for the night, and the Injun Cove (Cape Charles) neighborhood where I lived appeared dark and vacant. The house where I boarded was the only house with lights on, and thus the candidate's destination. The candidate introduced himself and chatted for a few minutes before boarding his boat for the journey back to Mary's Harbour. He may have suspected that he had visited all of Cape Charles!

The Progressive Conservative candidate held a well-attended election rally at the Cape Charles school. The candidate made a number of specific promises—to work for an improved fishery, lower food prices, improved transportation, and others, all issues of local concern.

On election day only about one-half of Cape Charles's eligible voters cast ballots. Twenty-seven voted for the P.C. candidate and seven for the Liberal. However, the Liberal won and represented the Eagle River riding until 1989.

Chapter 5

Religion, Beliefs, and Tradition

Virtually all Lodge Bay people are nominal Anglicans and organize their religious lives around the Christian calendar, observing the important Christmas, Lenten, and Easter seasons. The community has no permanent Anglican clergy and is served on a part-time basis by the minister stationed in Mary's Harbour. The minister occasionally visits and holds services in the small church at Cape Charles during summer. Lodge Bay had no church building in 1979, and religious services were conducted in the school. For several months during 1979, a representative of the Anglican Church Army was assigned to the Mary's Harbour parish and thus, Cape Charles and other summer stations received more frequent visits.

Formal Religion

I have emphasized the utility of Gemeinschaft in understanding various dimensions of Lodge Bay life. Here we need to mention an ideological expression of the Gemeinschaft—the Settler aversion to embrace difference, especially when it threatens local beliefs. By analogy, and at the risk of oversimplifying, recall how biologists describe genetic mutations as generally deleterious, in so far as they threaten the adaptation a species has with its environment. Similarly, during the past century and a half, Lodge Bay folk have come to terms with their environment and with each other. They are understandably wary about the introduction of new beliefs. In essence then, this ideological dimension of Gemeinschaft is conservative yet adaptive.

Regarding formal religion, one commonly hears the orthodox view that "what you're born you are . . . and there is nothing that should or could be done about it." Implicit here is the conviction that it is "normal" and "proper" to live one's life with the religion one is born into and that conversion to another sect is "unnatural."

It is this adaptive conservatism that explains why Lodge Bay folk have long been reluctant to embrace different religious practices, and have, on occasion, defended what they see as their formal religious turf. Historically, the Anglican Settlers reacted to occasional Roman Catholics and Methodists who entered the area. Irish immigration to southeastern Labrador occurred in the nineteenth century. Irish immigrants were often Roman Catholics with names like Spearing, Murphy, and Cumby, and settled in the Battle Harbour area. While most of these Catholics did eventually convert to Anglicanism, the fact that Battle Harbour–area Catholics and Anglicans buried their dead in separate cemeteries confirms that some denominational thinking existed.

One notable Roman Catholic fossilized in Lodge Bay lore is old Grannie Griffin. The Griffins, from Harbour Grace, Newfoundland, originally came as stationers to the Labrador coast between Camp Islands and Lodge Bay. They are remembered as impoverished people who first wintered at Cowhouse, then Lodge Bay, and finally Sound Brook (Simm's Bay—just south of Cape Charles). Grannie Griffin (née Sooley, Suly, or Sullivan) is said to have emigrated from Ireland. She married Michael Griffin and they raised at least three sons and two daughters. Folks remembered that Grannie suffered from cerebral palsy. She died about 1925 at Cape Charles and was buried on uninhabited Fox Island, near Injun Cove, Cape Charles. (The only visible grave stone in Fox Island's small cemetery is that of William Butt, remembered as a Methodist and the maternal grandfather of John Pye.) An older informant who witnessed Grannie Griffin's burial maintained that she had asked to be buried on Fox Island. Younger informants believe her burial there was necessary because there was no Catholic cemetery at Cape Charles. In any event, it is said that a large rock removed during excavation of the grave fell either accidentally or purposely on top of Grannie Griffin's casket. Several people told me that someone said, "she'll never get out of that."

Pentecostalism diffused to southeastern Labrador in the 1930s (Southard 1982, 168–169) and has successfully challenged the Anglican hegemony over the region. Lodge Bay folk oppose proselytism from competing religious denominations, again primarily because of the belief that one should remain what one was at birth. This belief became apparent to me in April 1979, when a

Pentecostal delegation from St. Lewis flew by private plane to Lodge Bay for a social visit. Rumors of their impending visit circulated well in advance, causing considerable speculation and consternation in the community. The visitors were welcomed by an affluent couple who were socially marginal, partially because they were not from Lodge Bay. I visited the couple and their guests for tea. The visiting Pentecostals enjoyed a safe haven at the couple's house. Present were three Lodge Bay people with relatives in St. Lewis. All were either sympathetic to Pentecostalism or actual church members. However, the delegation were clearly not welcome elsewhere. Their movements were closely monitored, albeit from a distance, and the visit was the major topic of conversation for several days.

Other local sectarian feelings are often subtle and symbolic. For example, one Lodge Bay man quipped that he disliked the use of green paint as trim on fish store houses or boats because it was "too Irish." Another man explained that red and grey were "our colors" for painting the inside of boats. In sum, like other small communities, Lodge Bay folk observe and reject differences that potentially upset the status quo. Difference, rather than religious differences, is threatening and spurned.

Folk Beliefs and Practices

In addition to beliefs about organized religion, Lodge Bay and other southeastern Labrador people adhere to a body of folk belief and customary practice that either developed locally or originated in the British Isles. These folk beliefs include stories of mysterious lights, mythical or heroic beings, and threatening supernatural figures. They are an expression of local culture communicating important moral and environmental lessons helpful for practical existence. Historically, such local lore served as a gripping course aimed at reminding each new generation of fishers, trappers, and hunters about the perils of the Labrador environment. Yet times have changed and younger villagers might be embarrassed by mention of such "old foolishness." Electric lights have brightened the lamp-lit kitchens where such lore once mesmerized listeners. Lodge Bay people now claim to prefer "the story" (afternoon television soap operas) to stories of "Ol' Smoker" and other supernatural characters. Yet elements of this lore and its functions persist.

Many of these beliefs have a supernatural basis; that is, they transcend natural processes and laws and are generally beyond human understanding and control. A second broad category of belief systems discussed below are cultural constructs without a supernatural basis. These are the rules by which people live, the cognitive system determining human action.

The majority of belief systems discussed here were observed and collected during fieldwork at Lodge Bay and Cape Charles. However, when relevant, my data is supplemented by that from other southeastern Labrador and Newfoundland communities. Much of this supplementary data is taken from the Memorial University of Newfoundland's Folklore and Language Archives (MUNFLA).

I have followed and indeed adapted the belief system classifications of folklorists Butler (1985) and Widdowson (1977). These classifications were developed to serve purposes different than my own; Butler's to categorize emic cognitive concepts and Widdowson's to inventory and analyze Newfoundland human and supernatural threatening figures. I also relate the Labrador narratives to Euroamerican folk motifs, principally Thompson's (1955) and Baughman's (1966) folk motif indices, and thus present this first attempt to systematically describe southeastern Labrador Settler folk beliefs in a community context.

Supernatural Beings

Butler's (1985) category of supernatural beings corresponds to Widdowson's (1977) broader Class A (supernatural, mythological, fictitious, and invented figures). Widdowson acknowledges that this is the largest and most difficult category to classify (103). Five subcategories of supernatural beings follow.

Diabolical Figures

Lodge Bay people once shared their world with a number of diabolical and threatening figures, some of which they associated with particular geographic locations. One frequently heard story concerns a brook near a place known as Cowhouse (south of Cape Charles), locally known as the place where the Devil dragged his tail. A rock near the brook has a groove in it, much as though a tail had scored it. (The imprint of various parts of the Devil's body, usually the foot, is common in Newfoundland folk narratives [Oliver 1970, Devil's footprints, Bonavista; Adams 1971, Devil's cloven hoof print, Red Island, Placentia Bay; Renouf 1971, Devil's well, Logy Bay]).

The story occurring at Cowhouse features an extraordinary meeting between an unusual woman named Polly and a figure locally assumed to have been the Devil. An informant explained:

There was an ol' Polly Griffin, she was a relation to Griffins, she was sort of a little bit retarded, eh? She had no fear. Now there's a place over there [Cowhouse] called "where the Devil dragged his tail," over in the *cosh* [brook], and this is where the Devil dragged his tail, a big trench, eh. That's what they used to call it. There's a water well there, right where the Devil dragged his tail at. So you wouldn't catch nobody goin' there in the night time to get water.

But this night they got a big shot of ducks, the Griffins. Now they wanted water and Geez, they never had guts enough to go and poor ol' Polly she had no fear. They said, "Polly, go out to the brook," she took the bucket, she went out. She didn't tell lies, she never told no lies, I mean she was that kind of person. 'Cause I heard Mom say, she had her one time, she used to work with her and she'd never tell no lies. And by 'n' by she [Polly] came back and [they] said, "Seen 'en Polly?" "Yes," she said, "I seen a man stuck up in the brook." [They] said, "What'd you do?" She said, "Move, sir, I likes me water." So he stepped to one side and she got her water and went on.

Polly's successful encounter with the man, whom several informants described as tall and dressed in black, partly explains the story's popularity. Moreover, the refusal of all except Polly to go to the well in the dark suggests that the place and its nightly caretaker must have been an effective mechanism for threatening both children and adults.

Another Lodge Bay devilish and threatening figure is the *Bullybagger*. Widdowson (1977, 189) interprets the Bullybagger as an invented figure. The Bullybagger is a devilish figure in the description provided by Lodge Bay people. I first learned about the Bullybagger from a young mother who, as her children listened, described him as a horned evil creature with big eyes and a pronged tail.

Lodge Bay people equate the Bullybagger with the *Byhalder*. Though I do not have a description of the Byhalder, the etymology of the word derives from "by" meaning "boy," and "hald" meaning "grab hold of." Children are warned, "Don't go down to the wharf now, or the Byhalder will have you." In keeping children away from wharfs, the Byhalder at Lodge Bay functions like the "Water Man" at Salmon Bight (Black Tickle). There, children venturing onto fishing stages are warned that the Water Man, said to live beneath fishing stages, might get them (James 1971, 14). Similarly, Lodge Bay children summering on Wall's Island, Cape Charles, were cautioned to remain near their homes, or else *Mother Wall* might get them.

Other threatening figures documented from the southeastern Labrador region include the "black man" and "boogie man" from Mary's Harbour (Mesher 1967) and the "boggie-man," "boo-man," and "gollie wogs" at Cartwright (Burdett 1967). Only one of these figures, the black man, appears to personify the Devil; the others belong in Widdowson's category of invented figures. Widdowson explains that the black man is a common euphemism for the Devil in Newfoundland oral tradition (1977, 112–115).

(Unnamed) Ghosts and Spirits

When in the spring of 1979 I announced my plans to board that summer in a particular Cape Charles house, some people cautioned me that the house was haunted (locally pronounced hanted). I would later learn that few of the many ghost stories set in this house feature "true ghosts" (H. Halpert, personal communication, 1980). As supernatural figures, true ghosts are manifestations of actual individuals who met tragic, violent, or unnatural deaths and who, for that reason, return to haunt particular people or places (Jones 1944; Montell 1975). In the following three ghost stories, the first two cases illustrate the potential for ghost belief; the second shows how ghost mythology encourages social control; and the third was perhaps a true ghost.

The first example is ordinarily told with levity and actually describes what folklorist Hubert Halpert calls a "ghost which wasn't a ghost" (personal communication, 1980). Significantly, the story is often told along with other ghost stories, sometimes by those wishing to prove that real ghosts (locally pronounced ghostess; singular ghost) do not exist. The story features three persons: Eva, the daughter of a man who once owned the house; Billy, her lover; and Hussey, an old Camp Island stationer fisher, whose memorable night at the Cape Charles house initiated the story. Laughing, my informant explained:

> Uncle Si had a daughter, Eva, she used to go with a fellow Bill Pelly, belonged to Carbonear. He used to . . . every chance he'd get he'd get in bed with her, eh. Now this ol' Hussey from the Camps [Islands], now he was Aunt Hettie's grandfather, now when he'd come down in the fall of the year, he'd stay there. So this' where they put 'em at, in Eva's bed. So Bill didn't know anything about it, so sometime in the night, the old fella told this now, Uncle Hussey he heard something come in, he said this man came in and put his hands all over his head, thought it was Eva see, frightened the shit out of the ol' fella.

A second example illustrates how ghost belief encourages appropriate social behavior. It is an example of what Halpert calls a false or "sham ghost," that is, when one person attempts to convince another of the presence of ghosts. The case involves two former occupants of the house, a woman and her mother-in-law. Apparently, the woman began accumulating too many household goods and property, much to the disgust of her mother-in-law and, presumably, others at Cape Charles. To counter her daughter-in-law's greed, the mother-in-law attempted to frighten her by rattling dishes and silverware, thereby exploiting the tradition that the house was in fact haunted. The mother-in- law's deception resembles Baughman's (1966, K 1887) motif of illusory sounds.

An informant described a third and final incident occurring in the alleged haunted house as a ghost story, though the identity of the ghost is unknown. The story involves three Lodge Bay men who were seal hunting at Cape Charles one autumn, when the settlement was vacant.

> I heard me father say, he've heard the ghosts and that . . . and this old fellow, Uncle Billy (Ol' Scuffs'), he owned it [the house] in the first place. He died. Now Uncle Si, his son . . . they used to have a post office now in Billy's time, Aunt Clara [operated it], I think it was. So they was out there sealin' in the fall of the year, and they stayed there and sometime in the night they heard someone come up, scuffin' up over the [fishing] flake [in front of the house] and they [i.e., the ghost] come in through . . . [the door]. There was three of 'em there, the three of them sleeping in the one room. So there was only two of 'em heard it now, the other fellow was asleep, Uncle Si was asleep. Bob Howard, that's who it was. So by 'n' by they [i.e., the ghost] come in, they opened the door and they went in to the post office part . . . and you could hear 'em rattlin' over the letters and haulin' open the drawers and whatever he was lookin' for, he got and he went on 'or through, scuffed down 'or the bank again.

Another example involves a "true ghost" whose identity is central to the story's moral. The case is reported to have occurred in recent times, in a southeastern Labrador community north of Lodge Bay. A man began having an affair with a woman while his wife lay dying. Following the wife's death, it is said that the man and his lover began seeing the ghost of his wife, usually on the porch of their former home. Not insignificantly, many people question the veracity of these sightings, claiming they are only made up by people in the community. This story resembles Baughman's (1966, E 221.1) motifs in which (a) the dead wife haunts her husband on his second marriage and (b) in which the dead wife torments her husband who has let her die of neglect (1966, E 221.5). Even if only made up, the story illustrates how ghost belief may be used to enforce social norms, in this case regarding marital fidelity and proper care of sick spouses.

Phantom Sounds, Lights, and Fireballs

In a community where hunting and trapping have long been important one might suspect that people would be accustomed to the sound of gunshots. However, the community's small size, effective interhousehold oral communication system, and, particularly in the past, relationship among individuals and specific hunting/trapping territories, led to a shared understanding as to where other hunters and trappers were likely to be at any given time. Hence, strange or unexplained gunshots might be attributed to supernatural causes. Locals usually associate such gunshots with ghosts, inadvertent trespassing on another person's property, or immediate and potentially hazardous changes in weather. In recalling one such unexplained gunshot, an informant explained,

> Now another time me and poor [now deceased] Sol me brother was [camped] in the Lodge Pond [west of Lodge Bay]. Them times I mean there wasn't no people goin' round like there is now. This was in the fall of the year, in October month, the pond wasn't even froze up. We got in the [canvas tent] camp in the night and had a couple of partridges cooked and we got our supper. So [we] just laid back in the bunk and by 'n' by "bang" goes a shotgun or a rifle, don't know what it was, by 'n' by "bang" goes another, three. Now I was kind of a little bit . . . wasn't thinkin' 'bout a ghost now. Now what I thought was we built a new camp up there the year before that and we used to have a camp down the foot of the pond. We had the camp up the head of the pond then I thought something happened and someone come in and didn't know where the camp was at and fired their gun to let us know, you know? So it was a nice moonlight night and we dodged down the pond and hollered out and bawled out, never heard nothin' . . . Now poor Sol he was more nervous, eh, he believed in ghosts so he was up all night but I went back and went to sleep. Now before we went to sleep, wasn't in camp before long, before "bang" two more shots goes. And we never 'er found what that was.

Another informant recounted the same story and clearly associated the mysterious gunshots with the stormy weather that followed. One may conclude then that mysterious gunshots are harbingers of danger though determination of the type of danger depends on context.

Phantom light stories have been widely reported in Labrador (Junek 1937, 83; Ford, 1977), Newfoundland (Widdowson 1977), and elsewhere in Atlantic Canada (Creighton 1988). Phantom lights are also associated with fairy lore in parts of Newfoundland (Casey 1967). In Lodge Bay and the region generally, however, phantom lights are primarily associated with death. Many people claim to have seen such lights moving along the surface of water, ice, or land to a place where someone is known to have drowned, frozen to death, or met another untimely end. There, the light goes out.

An excellent example of this is the often told story of lights being seen on a bay south of the community, where the Hunt brothers went through the ice and drowned during the winter of 1927. Perhaps because of the relative youth of the brothers (ages 17 and 21), because of historic marriages and other social ties between their kin and Lodge Bay people, and because they had been courting in Lodge Bay, narratives of this old tragedy persist. I maintain that the telling of stories involving phantom lights also serves to reiterate the dangers of travel over water and sea ice.

One Lodge Bay man associated phantom lights with death and bad weather:

> Now I've seen lights lots of times, you know, ahead of storms and stuff like that. There's a grave over there [near Cowhouse] on Carrol's Cove Point. When I was going there trappin' I've seen lights on that grave in the night time, I mean it was impossible for anyone to be there but I've seen lights on that grave. [Anthropologist: What did they look like?] Well, it's always before a storm, just a light.

Others attempt scientific explanations of phantom lights. For example, such explanations would attribute sightings of the light on Carrol's Cove Point to certain atmospheric conditions, particularly those leading to a southerly wind. Accordingly, the actual light seen during such conditions is beyond the point, on the northeast corner of Belle Isle!

Although not as common as stories about phantom lights, I also collected the following story about strange balls of fire or light.

> Lots of times you see balls of fire in the sky, I suppose you've seen that yourself. One time when I was a young fellow, I don't know who was with me, we was walking down from the Cove [at Cape Charles] down to the Tickle. And the moon was up and we looked up and we seen . . . just like the moon, a big red ball on the horizon and we said, "two moons, that's funny." We didn't know the difference and by 'n' by he burst, and he went in a million pieces . . . That's what they claim, some kind of a ball of fire . . . That was in the fall.

The Kerrymen, Ghosts of the Ancestors

One kind of narrative I collected at Lodge Bay is regionally restricted to the coast between Lodge Bay and Henley Harbour. It features the Kerrymen, a fabled ancestral population who, in the words of one informant, "must have been the earliest settlers." As ghosts of the ancestors, the Kerrymen are also guardians of ancestral property. To understand the Kerrymen one must know that there are a number of historic homestead and settlement ruins in the area. No one knows who built these and when. One informant explained,

> There's what they call the Kerrymen, you ever hear talk of 'em? They's ol' fellas that used to live there, years ago and all these ol' paths, no one knows where they come from and they claims ol' Kerrymen used to live there. So if you happen to build a house over this path, you'd always have trouble, eh.

The same informant illustrated the Kerryman belief by saying,

> Now Grandfather Hunt and dad, I heard dad tellin' this hisself, now Grandfather Hunt's not afraid of much of anything, now they was in around a place called Cowhouse Droke once, cuttin' sticks. Now, they had a team of dogs with 'em. And by 'n' by they heard a shot and there was no one there. Grandfather Hunt grabbed the ax and said, "Lord Geez, someone tried to shoot us" and every dog stuck their ears up and he said, "I thin' the best thing we can [do is] get out of this." And they only got not very far and the worst storm they had for the winter.

The two men were cutting wood on a path attributed to the Kerrymen and in their case the misfortune that followed the mysterious gunshots was a bad storm.

Opinions vary on the disposition and behavior of the Kerrymen. For example one informant explained that the Kerrymen function as threat figures to prevent children from wandering into the woods. However, most people characterize the Kerrymen as harmful only when people alter or trespass on their paths, even unintentionally. In this sense, the Kerrymen may influence adult behavior as much as that of children. The element of Kerryman lore that prohibits use of ancestral property, resembles J. C. Davis's (1977, 42–43) account of a Table Bay house inadvertently built where two long abandoned and invisible paths cross. The unusual happenings observed at the Table Bay house finally required that the house be dismantled and rebuilt elsewhere. Similarly, I suggest that as potentially malevolent ghosts of unknown ancestors, the Kerrymen remind the living of ancient and long-forgotten property, and by inference, inform each generation that the living must respect the property of the dead. I am not aware of whatever relationship may exist between the Kerrymen and Kerry Cove (near George's Cove, see map 2). The Kerrymen may draw their name from Irish migration to the area during the last century. One assumes some connection with County Kerry, Ireland, and if this is so, the Kerrymen may not be so much the ancestors but more an expression of denominationalism, the Catholic Other on this largely Anglican coast. If so, traversing their ancient grounds risks another kind of contamination.

Kerryman lore also resembles fairy and so-called path lore (see Rieti 1991; Narváez 1987). Grenfell reported a great belief in fairies on the coast, but by the time of my fieldwork little such belief appears to have survived. My impression is supported by a comment made by Sandwich Bay Settler Henry John Williams, following his short description of troublesome but harmless fairies near Cartwright (Williams 1979, 4). Williams added that "there don't be no fairy stories now like there used to be." The sole reference related to fairy lore that I collected was that a man reported getting "*fairy headed*" and was temporarily unable to move. This corresponds to Baughman's (1966, F 377) motif, a supernatural lapse in time in fairyland. Being fairy headed resembles Newfoundland references to being "fairy led" (Verge 1967) or "fairy struck" (Gushue 1968, 152). In such cases, a person venturing into the woods might be spirited away by fairies and following such an episode, may have a starry gaze in his or her eyes (Jacobs 1967).

Two Named Phantasmic Figures

Two final named supernatural beings are Ol' Smoker and Jack O' the Lantern. Accounts of Ol' Smoker have been reported from many parts of the southeastern Labrador coast (Burdett 1979, 5) and from northern Newfoundland (Halpert, personal communication, 1980). The origins of Ol' Smoker lore may be related to one meaning of "smoke" in the Newfoundland and Labrador lexicon, in which wind-driven rain or snow is said to "smoke" (Story, Kirwin, and Widdowson 1982, 498). The legend of Ol' Smoker resembles Stith Thompson's (1955–58, D 285.1) motif of a person transformed to smoke. Alternatively, the roots of smoker lore may run deeper in the region's social history. As recently as the early twentieth century and to the north of Lodge Bay lived an Inuit family named Smoker. Quite possibly, Ol' Smoker as stranger may be an analogue of Inuit as stranger.

Lodge Bay people are equivocal about whether Ol' Smoker or Jack 'O the Lantern are threatening. Of the two figures, narratives describing Ol' Smoker are more common. Smoker is described as an unidentified man lost in a snow storm who is occasionally seen driving a dog team of five or eight dogs. After any person has first seen Smoker, they are always somehow prevented from positively identifying what they have just seen. An informant described one sighting as follows:

> Well, there was a fella one time come up here [Lodge Bay], up the bay, somewhere, he had five or eight dogs, he got caught in a snowstorm and he was lost and no one ever heard talk of him after. So, now I always heard the yarn about Smoker . . . he was dressed up in a white kind of suit, and he had five white dogs, and . . . Now one time me and me father was driving up the bay here and we looked up and we seen this fella coming down, right fer us, he had five white dogs and a load of boughs [branches] on . . . Dad said, "That's the one now, hauling down a load of boughs for something . . ." He drove right over on the broad side of us. It was all light snow, wasn't hard you could see . . . So whatever happened, two of the [our] dogs got hooked up and we took our eyes off to see what happened to the dogs. And we looked and buddy was gone and we went [over] and there was no track. Two of us seen that!

When I questioned his sighting, the informant added, "I looked at the old man who said, 'That's Smoker, I've seen he thousands of times.'"

Jack O' the Lantern (or Jack o' Lantern) narratives occur throughout the island of Newfoundland (Widdowson 1977, 131–137). A Lodge Bay man who claimed to have seen Jack O' the Lantern described him as follows: "He's the fella who goes around with the lantern. People see him and by 'n' by he'll rise up, he'll go on over the hills." This description of Jack O' the Lantern lacks the threatening or malevolent associations inherent in variants presented by Widdowson (1977). This may have been because of the social context of the interview (namely, anthropologist and adult male informant) as much as with the local meaning of Jack O' the Lantern. In other contexts, including the presence of children, the relationship between Jack O' the Lantern and the dangers of straying into the hills near the community may be stressed. However, two similarities with Widdowson's variants may be noted. First, the necessarily nocturnal time of sightings and second, potential similarities between the levitation (over the hills) in the Lodge Bay version and associative explanations of phosphorescent marsh gases typical of the Newfoundland versions (Widdowson 1977, 131–132).

"Strange" Human Beings

This category borrows from Widdowson's Class B in that it is "typified by living people" who are temporarily or permanently considered abnormal, unusual, or strange (1977, 227).

Janneying

Janneying, or mummering, as in other parts of Newfoundland and Labrador, in Lodge Bay occurs during the twelve days of Christmas between Christmas Day or Boxing Day (26 December) and the Feast of Epiphany (6 January). I was not in Lodge Bay at that time and thus did not observe janneying. However, Lodge Bay people describe janneying in festive tones. Many continue to practice the custom, dressing up in unfamiliar clothing and wearing masks. They visit from house to house, where hosts attempt to guess their identity. *Janneys* are then rewarded with edibles or more often alcoholic beverages before moving on to another house.

Like other customary practices, janneying varies somewhat between communities within the region. At Henley Harbour (Clark 1978, 7), Cartwright (Burdett 1967), and probably elsewhere, janneys carry a split (a small piece of firewood or kindling) or stick, perhaps to disguise the familiar sound of their knocks on neighbors' doors (Clark 1986, 9). At least at Cartwright, Janneys are said to sing noisily between households and react assertively to anyone trying to expose their identity. When Janneys knock on doors at Mary's Harbour, they ask stock questions such as "Any janneys allowed in?" Householders respond with questions such as "Where are you from?" To which the janneys answer, "The moon," "North pole," and so on (Mesher 1967). Once inside the house, janneys are expected to entertain by dancing and singing, while householders try removing their costumes, in order to ascertain their identity (Davis 1967). Following their performance, janneys at Henley Harbour were given Christmas cake topped with bakeapple or blackberry syrup (Clark 1978).

Strangers

While they are janneying, janneys are symbolic strangers (Clark 1986, 10), but communities are periodically visited by real strangers. As Conrad Arensberg ([1937] 1988) so candidly observes on his arrival in Luogh, Ireland, the arrival of a stranger in any small community is an important event. From the perspective of the stranger, people are friendly and polite, but cautious. As in many small communities the arrival of strangers kindles gossip and attempts to identify his or her purpose for being there. A former resident of Battle Harbour recalls that when strangers arrived there, people peered through their windows, speculating about their identity and intentions (Corbett 1976, 16). In Lodge Bay, at least initially, parents used my presence to warn their children, just as they might use police or another authority figure (Walsh 1967). By representing what the community is not, strangers unwittingly possess the power to help elders steer children toward desired ends.

Lodge Bay oral tradition contains a category of lore describing exploitation by passing strangers, usually Newfoundlanders. Many such narratives describe collectors of curios, who are said to have purchased most of the community's old "muzzle loaders" (rifles), often for little or nothing. And then there was "Dr." Moses Earle, Carbonear snake-oil salesman. The good doctor arrived unannounced at Cape Charles one summer in the late 1920s or early 1930s, selling a medicinal tonic that he concocted on location. Aunt Susan was hired to help Earle mix the tonic and remembers that it was composed largely of eggs. Lacking cash, one ailing local exchanged two ancient family pictures, set in oblong curly maple frames, for two bottles of the worthless tonic. Informants were happy to add that sometime later, Moses Earle was arrested in Newfoundland for smuggling liquor.

People from Cartwright told me about a Newfoundland vessel, the *Sandy Point*, which had been collecting scrap metal along the coast during the mid-1960s. The vessel was heavily laden and people advised its unusual crew (a man and his wife, another woman, and a dog!) not to leave, as a storm was approaching. Ignoring these warnings, the ship disembarked and was never seen again. Its nameplate and some clothing were later found in the vicinity of Table or Partridge Bay, south of Cartwright. People added that the strangers had dealt only in cash, but that no cash was ever found.

Unusual Locations, Natural and Unexplainable Phenomena

While some of the locations mentioned by Widdowson—cemeteries and root crop cellars (1977, 307–308) are occasionally frightening to Lodge Bay young (and old), what strikes me as more fascinating are places where unusual events are believed to regularly occur.

There is a direct relationship between the extent to which people fear certain places and the extent to which they believe in ghosts and other unexplainable phenomena. As we have seen, Lodge Bay people associate locations such as Cowhouse, Camp Islands, Spirit Cove, and Cape Charles (particularly Injun Cove) with unusual experiences, much as Oscar Junek's (1937) Blanc Sablon settlers did with Greenly Islands, and Cartwright people do with Seal Islands, which they claim is the "real ghost place" of that area.

A number of people who claim *not* to believe in ghosts do believe in *tokens*, foreboding portents of future events or impending death. While many sensual stimuli—sounds, smells, visions, lights, animals or strange people—can be interpreted as tokens, Lodge Bay people primarily use the term to refer to two categories of stimuli. In the first, the unexpected sound of an unseen animal is associated with a person's death. The actual association between the sound and death is made after learning of the death. Narratives describing this kind of token are ordinarily communicated in the third person; that is, they describe an incident experienced by someone the informant knew, rather than himself or herself. In one example, an older informant recalled that he and several others were once camping near Burton's Pond (near Lodge Bay) and, at daybreak, he suddenly heard a flapping or rustling sound, like an eagle landing, behind him. He surmised it must have been an owl landing and added that later that day, he learned that a woman died at Henley Harbour.

Another informant explained how a Lodge Bay man and others once heard a rooster crow the same day the man's father died. The informant added that at the time, "There wasn't a rooster within a hundred miles!" Roosters crowing after dark are also tokens of death in parts of Newfoundland (Payne 1964).

Another example of a token involving animals occurred when a Lodge Bay couple was just married and wintering in Carbonear, Newfoundland. They were living in a large house where a rat had been seen. The incident occurred one night as the couple were going to bed. The husband was already in bed, and as the wife approached the bed, she experienced an unseen but audible "force" at her feet, which she said ran around her three times and sounded like a scratching or shuffling sound. Seconds later, it could be distinctly heard descending the stairs. The husband believes it was a rat though for the wife, the meaning of the mysterious force was revealed the next morning, when she learned that her mother had died back in Labrador. The fact that the "force" encircled the woman's legs three times corresponds to the common association between death and the number three (Thompson 1955–58, D 1273.1.1.3).

In the second type of token, a person hears the voice of a deceased person simultaneously with the time of their death. Such tokens are usually described in the first person. For example, "It happened to me one time. Well like somebody dyin' belong to you and they're thinkin' about you when they're dyin' or they want to see you, you know. Well . . . you can see, I don't know about see' em, you can hear 'em." The man continued,

> 'Cause I had a sister died now, only young, sixteen I suppose. We knew she was dyin' but didn't know when she'd die. I was going over Long Pond Droke, setting rabbit snares, I was only young. But, oh, I got down to the Droke and I got astray and by 'n' by I heard someone sing out to me, like a woman's voice. And I made it was her, I could tell it was her voice. You know, I got kinda scared and you know I couldn't get no headway, you know there's places you get you know *fairyhead*. I know what that is, you couldn't pick yourself up. I was a long while before I picked myself up, so when I got across the Dogberry Hill, I met up with Si Pye, come looking for me, said she'd died a few minutes before that and when I got home she was singing out to me her last breath.
>
> So that's the reason I believe in that 'en and mother told me that the last word she said was singing out to me. I was the only one who wasn't home, eh. She wanted to see me, I was the only one, they'd say, "He'd be here the once." That was the last word she said.

Tokens are an excellent example of the unseen, sympathetic threads uniting Lodge Bay folk, the telepathic expression of Gemeinschaft. After all, how else can one explain the immediate sensing of a distant loved one's death?

Buried Treasure

Buried treasure is locally thought to be guarded, frequently by a ghostly caretaker who serves for a specific time period, after which the treasure may be safely discovered and used. The ghostly caretaker corresponds with Baughman's motif (1966, E 291.2.1), ghost in human form guarding treasure. A Lodge Bay man said,

> We often heard tell of money and treasure buried down around the islands and up around Camp Islands. Now I believe it was Captain Cook or Captain . . . er or one of those pirates . . . he buried this treasure up around Big Duck Island, I always heard tell of that.

He explained how caretakers assumed their roles.

> I used to read these books you know, pirate money, they'd bury this money and then they'd say, "Who'll volunteer to look after it?" And by 'n' by some poor fool would say "I will," and as soon as he did they'd shoot 'en. Well now, he's the fellow looks after the money.

Finally, he explained what happened when a caretaker had fulfilled his mandate.

> One time me father and his brother was birdin'. They was passin' along by Spirit Cove and they seen this man passin' along the hill and becken' to 'em. They thought some fella got stranded on the island. And they went in and he jumped aboard the boat and almost put the head of the boat in under . . . and he beckoned them over the other side, never spoke, and they thought it funny, you know. Now w'er they made up this or it's true I don't know but I've heard 'em tellin' it so they claims that after that the money was got.

Talk of buried treasure also occurs in the vicinity of Battle Harbour. Around 1970 a sailboat is said to have come into St. Lewis Inlet and those aboard are said to have gone ashore at Red Island, carrying shovels. They left hurriedly two days later and locals believe they must have found something (Corbett 1976). Rumors also exist about buried treasure or of a dead baby buried on Big Island (ibid.).

Weather Lore

There are several examples of what I shall call weather lore. One man explained how one only had two weeks each month to cut wood. He said one should never cut logs after a full moon, as the wood would shrink. Thus, one had two weeks (between a new moon and a full moon) to cut, a time period he called the "growin' of the moon." However, most weather lore relates one natural event to future changes in weather. Thus, for example, "If it rains on the third day of the month or snows or whatever the weather is, it will be like that for the rest of the month" (obtained from an eighty-six-year-old former Lodge Bay native—Pye 1984, 8)

The following exemplifies the persistence of such beliefs. A thirty-eight-year-old Lodge Bay man said if one hangs the head of a wolf, every time the wind changes the head will turn windward (toward the wind direction). Dr. Wilfred Grenfell records the existence of this custom in early twentieth-century Labrador. He writes that a

> fox's or wolf's head [is] suspended by a cord from the center, and . . . will always twist the way from which the wind is going to blow. One man had a barometer of this kind hanging from his roof, and explained that the peculiar fact was due to the nature of the animals, which in life always went to windward of others; but if you had a seal's head similarly suspended, it would turn from the wind, owing to the timid character of that creature. (1919, 143)

And there are many more examples of predicting a change in wind or weather. For example, an old man in Lodge Bay forecasted that there would be a change in wind because his bones ached and that codfish had begun moving into his son's cod trap. The same man opined to have never seen a codfish taken in a cod trap during a northeast wind. A Henley Harbour woman told me that "if the moon is quartered, if it is shaped like a powder horn, or tippy, it is a sure sign they'd be bad weather."

Another harbinger of changing weather is *sun hounds*. A sun hound is a ring around the sun with an opening in it resembling a rainbow. Sun hounds may be seen any time of day. Lodge Bay people say that if the opening is to the westward, there is going to be wind. (For other descriptions of sun hounds, see Story, Kerwin, and Widdowson 1982, 542.)

The Ritual Organization of Time

This category includes taboos and regimen regulating the uses of time. Among them are taboos against work on Sundays, Lenten taboos, and the schedule of daily meals.

Sunday was once a day of rest. One older woman explained that until about the 1940s, people observed strict taboos against work on Sundays. On Saturday evening, people would peel all the potatoes, turnips, and other vegetables for the Sunday dinner. On Sunday evening, they would wash their dishes, leaving the boilers and pans to be washed Monday. Even today, this same woman will not knit on Sundays. She explained that during World War II, she and other women knitted sweaters as part of the war effort. One Sunday she took the unusual action of trying to complete a sweater sleeve so that the sweater could be taken to Battle Harbour the next day for shipping. After completing the sweater, she discovered she had done one part incorrectly; it had to be unraveled and was not ready for shipping. Since this incident she has never knitted on Sundays.

This woman's husband, once an avid trapper, illustrated his abstinence from work on Sunday by recalling that one Sunday an otter surfaced right in front of his Lodge Bay house, yet he would not shoot it. Nowadays, he may occasionally check his rabbit snares on Sundays—"just to get out of the house."

Many Lodge Bay folk observe the forty-day Lenten season preceding Easter. Meat and fat are not consumed on Ash Wednesday. In 1979 on the night preceding Ash Wednesday a number of the young men pledged to abstain from liquor, beer, and "smokes" during lent. Although they did so lightheartedly, while drinking, their pledges had a testimonial character. On Good Friday, people abstain from work either in the morning or, more commonly, all day. One man now living in Lodge Bay but originally from a nearby community, said he had never worked on Good Friday. He explained, "I don't know, it was just the way I was raised . . . I don't know if I'm any better for it." People also abstain from eating butter or fat on Good Friday; salt salmon is the common meal of that day.

As elsewhere in Newfoundland and Labrador, Lodge Bay people once consumed foods according to a remarkably regimented schedule. The rigidity of the schedule meant that each day's menu functioned almost like a calendar and doubtless served as a method of ordering time. Subject to availability, the daily main midday meal (dinner) was: Mondays (beans), Tuesdays (*cooked dinner*), Wednesdays (fish and *brewis*, pronounced brews, a plain hard bread, soaked and cooked with salt codfish), Thursdays (again, cooked dinner), Fridays (fish, cooked any style), Saturdays (pea soup), Sundays (fish and brewis for breakfast and cooked dinner). Informants emphasized that the menu for Tuesdays, Thursdays, and Sundays survives today.

Cultural Assumptions and Values

A number of cultural assumptions and values of Lodge Bay people are implicit in the beliefs and practices just presented. Those not so far addressed are also of interest.

Lodge Bay people face continuous dilemmas, whether to pursue personal or communal goals, whether to meet individual needs (including those of the family) or those of all Lodge Bay people. All need first to feed, clothe, and house themselves, but the small and closely knit scale of Lodge Bay overshadows each person's deliberations concerning the extent to which he or she pursues his or her own ends or those of the community. The highest prestige is accorded to those consistently willing and able to give more to the community than they take from it, people who work hard and effectively, are prosperous yet humble, and who have a pride in place and in the products they produce. These values—independence and individualism, coupled with a strong sense of responsibility to others—are enduring. For here is a timeless way of life closely attuned to the changing seasons, in which people individually know the most intimate details of their peers, where one's word still has meaning, and in which the etiquette of daily rituals reinforces continuity. But this lifestyle is increasingly under assault, complicating each person's deliberations concerning "me" or "they."

Individuals are identified and evaluated on several levels. At one level, all recognize old Uncle John, with his characteristic manner and idiosyncrasies. At another level, he is grouped with his immediate family, the John Pyes, and at a broader level, with a certain "race," "lot," or "crowd" of kin, usually having the surname Pye (see also Faris 1972). She or he may be renowned as a *hard* person or described more affectionately as being *not too easy*. This latter characterization normally refers to the diversity and high quality of a person's accomplishments.

Being considered a hard person may or may not be complimentary. For example, Henry Hunt is remembered as a hard man. His grandson recalled that Henry was,

> Always a hard man, you know, he had an awful temper, he'd do anything. . . . He was a hard ticket, you know when he was up around Camp Islands, there was nothing that could get ahead of 'en . . . He came home sometimes and he'd beat up the dishes and he'd beat up everything . . . [after one such session, his wife said to him], "You'll come to a bad end."

> One morning [years later, in Corner Brook] he went to church, came back from church and, ah he picked up his razor, no he went to the [medicine] shelf, he had heart trouble or something and they thought he might be getting his pills. So, Aunt Lil was making a pudding and by 'n' by some spots of the blood starts to come down through the loft. And they went up and he was like this [extended] and his throat was cut from here to here [pointing just under his ears]. And they said, "What'd you do?" Ah he [Henry] shook his head and he kicked and kicked and all the life went out of him.

The same informant compared Henry Hunt with another hard man, a Newfoundland fishing skipper named Sonny Marshall.

> Marshall and his men were hauling a cod trap one day when a shareman suddenly dropped dead from a heart attack. Marshall then took the dead man and shoved him up in the cuddy and that's all he thought about it—hauled away at his [cod] trap. He put away a big load of fish and by 'n' by another man picked up and said, "What are you going to bury that [dead man] or what?"

Of course not all hard persons commit suicide or ignore the dead. A milder variation of hardness is that of the label "hard case." A parent or close relative might use this phrase to refer to an incorrigible (usually male) child. On the other hand, a more distant relative or unrelated person would probably evaluate the same child more negatively. Social proximity masks one's evaluation.

A hard man may be respected if his bravery is considered daring, but not if it is reckless. Recklessness, particularly if it results in accidents to property or person, is scorned. Patience and tenacity are valued. While patience is a virtue, a person who is commonly *on the hook* or agitated, is negatively evaluated. In a society where immediate yet painstaking repairs to a broken chainsaw or outboard engine or the judgment to await improved weather before proceeding are commonplace, it is understandable why perseverance and predictability, rather than volatility, are valued.

Such traits as cleverness or musical ability are admired, particularly when they are used to serve the common good. Men and women are evaluated according to their adherence to customs shared by the community. Women have authority over their homes and are assessed by how well they keep them. For example, women place a clean tablecloth over the table before each meal and "lunch." Informants claimed that setting fresh tablecloths was a very old custom, dating back a hundred or more years. The practice persists even though other old customs, such as taboos against working on Sundays or the rafting of firewood, have faded.

The community allows few secrets. Children go from house to house at the end of the school year displaying their report cards. If however, a person's "secret" is discovered and it is believed she or he sought to deny the community's access to it, then the secret may be publicized as gossip. For example, a Mary's Harbour bachelor was the topic of gossip for several days because he flew to St. Anthony, Newfoundland, to cash a check in order not to reveal the selling price of a snowmobile.

Whatever their personal or familial characteristics, Lodge Bay/Cape Charles people unite in their awareness of belonging. In fact, when people mention other southeastern Labrador communities, they are often critical. Such talk most often refers to nearby Mary's Harbour, the community increasingly important to Lodge Bay. One man who lived in Mary's Harbour for a couple of years after relocating from another winter community, justified his preference for Lodge Bay by pointing to the forests surrounding the community. Others criticize the impersonal character of Mary's Harbour social life, the excessive benefits it receives from government, and so on. Even so, one cannot make too much of this differentiation: Lodge Bay people visit Mary's Harbour regularly to shop or to attend the Grenfell clinic; the two communities are also bridged by ties of blood and marriage.

Lodge Bay people do not consider the differences between

themselves and Mary's Harbour people as racial or ethnic. Yet their adaptive conservatism may be seen when discussing other, more distant communities. I have already mentioned how some people are concerned about increased marriages between their sons and daughters and St. Lewis spouses. This concern is partially based on racial or ethnic grounds—that is, the legacy of aboriginal ancestry still visible in some St. Lewis people. As one Lodge Bay man remarked, "Most all those people in Fox Harbour [St. Lewis] . . . you can tell . . . I don't know if it's Eskimos or Indians or what in the hell it is."

He continued to discuss native ancestry evident in Settlers further north: "After you pass this [Lodge Bay] and start to go north, you'll see a difference right away . . . even Cartwright, Rigolet, Port Hope Simpson . . . It's only here and Mary's Harbour . . . you won't find any . . . [native blood]."

Lodge Bay people view people in communities from St. Lewis north as "native." One Lodge Bay person, reluctant to acknowledge their aboriginal ancestry, flew to Goose Bay and on returning, was delayed in Cartwright because of bad weather. When telling me about this weather delay the person mentioned a previous incident in which some people are alleged to have gone into the lounge of a coastal boat docked in Cartwright and to have caused some damage. Irritated by the inconvenience of this weather delay, the person described the people that did the damage as being "just like savages . . . a bunch of half-breeds. . . ."

This Lodge Bay person's disparaging comments must be placed in context. Prior to the formation of aboriginal political groups, some Settlers with obvious aboriginal physical characteristics felt stigmatized and over compensated for such feelings of inferiority by rhetorically distancing themselves from *those* natives (Kennedy, 1982; Plaice, 1990).

The presumed racial or ethnic differences Lodge Bay people associate with communities from St. Lewis north, may of course be objectively explained by the social history of the region. Historically, the Battle Harbour area formed the northern periphery of a microregion focused toward the south, rather than north. Communication by coastal boat was between Corner Brook and Battle Harbour. Lodge Bay people married spouses from Battle Harbour, Henley Harbour, Camp Islands, and latterly Red Bay, as well as from Newfoundland. Only in recent years have Lodge Bay people visited and married persons from St. Lewis north.

Egalitarianism

Egalitarianism sets the tone of social interaction and people tend to understate or denigrate their notable accomplishments with phrases like "it's not too bad." Yet, rumors have always existed about the wealth of certain individuals, particularly those owning small retail shops. Moreover, I collected some data suggesting that leveling mechanisms, such as stealing and *scoffs*, function to redistribute wealth. One may with Gerald Sider (1986) interpret the incident to follow as symbolic protests by an underclass against their local merchant or, as the locals might see them, merely as insignificant pranks.

The term scoff is used in a manner compatible with Sider's (1986) examination of James Faris (1972), that is, as a meal of bucked or stolen food. An informant described an incident that occurred over fifty years ago.

> I've heard Dad talk about it . . . they'd be fishing Saturday evenings in the summer, coming towards fall of the year. Three or four of 'em would get in a big ol' boat and oar and they'd row up here in the bay and have a scoff. Hot supper. And they wouldn't have nothing only what they steal because . . . they had thousands o' it but they had to steal it for it to be any good, see? That was their make up then, see.

> And I heard 'em talking about ol' Soper [a Newfoundland merchant] you know, used to live up there in Watering Cove [Cape Charles]. He had a business up there. I mean them times they had plenty of everything and to have a hot supper, they'd go around to someone's garden, swipe the greens. And then they'd go up to ol' Soper and a couple of young fellows they'd go in talking to him and another fellow'd be in taking the beef and pork out of the barrel, you know [laughing]. You done that now, I suppose you'd be put in jail.

Others recalled a similar incident, also decades ago, in which young Lodge Bay men bored a hole through the floor of Soper's store into his rum barrel.

The Past in the Present

One January night brothers Raymond and Peter Hunt were returning by dog team from an evening in Lodge Bay to their winter homestead in Cowhouse. Raymond, aged seventeen, and Peter, aged twenty-one, had been courting in the community they knew well; before moving to Cowhouse, the Hunt family had wintered along the St. Charles River until the death of the boys' mother, Julia. Suddenly, as their dog team pulled them across frozen Simm's Bay there was a crash, then open water, throwing the brothers off their komatik into the icy water. They likely floundered in confusion, then yielded to the frozen sea and slipped beneath the surface. Their dogs crawled back onto the bay ice and remained obediently.

The next day Henry Hunt searched for his two sons, eventually espying the dog team and the deadly opening from atop a high hill overlooking the bay. Assuming tragedy at once, their father proceeded to Lodge Bay, where in anguish and grief he cried out for help. Men and youths hurried to harness dog teams. Some headed to Simm's Bay, others to Cape Charles to get a boat and codfish jiggers. The men worked quickly to retrieve the bodies. There was (surprisingly) little current beneath the hole, and the two wet corpses were soon jigged to the surface, covered with canvas, and taken to Lodge Bay. The corpses were laid out in the abandoned house where the boys had once lived, on the wooded banks of the St. Charles River. Two teenage Lodge Bay boys were asked to go to the house and light a fire in the wood stove. One lifted the canvas covering a corpse, either by mistake (as he told me) or out of curiosity, but dropped it at once—sea lice had eaten the face of one brother. The brothers were buried three days later.

I believe it significant that the Hunt brothers drowned in 1927, more than fifty years prior to my time in Lodge Bay; yet people told me several versions of the tragedy, each with different details. Such stories or gossip construct a continuous, living history of small villages. Like John Berger's (1979) French peasants, Lodge Bay people—both old people and the school children whose versions of the past I recorded—have a keen interest in their past (for a chronology of local history, see appendix 2). What is the significance of the past? Reference to some of the vast work on oral tradition helps answer this question.

Lodge Bay (like many small communities) is largely an oral culture, with different characteristics than literate cultures (people are also literate, but orality is more crucial to local communication). Distinguishing oral from literate cultures, Walter Ong (1982) observes that oral cultures tend to be more conservative; to deal less with abstractions than with concrete realities; never to tell narratives the same way twice; and so on. Clearly, many stories about the past ("gossip" [Berger 1979] or "historical gossip" [Vasina 1985]) serve contemporary purposes (Berger 1979; Ong 1982, 46). Oral tradition helps a community define itself, and to survive (Berger 1979) generating a "community portrait" (ibid., 9) or "community of memory" (Bellah et al., 1985). In defining what a community is, oral tradition also distinguishes it from the world beyond its boundaries, including neighboring communities.

I noted two themes in Lodge Bay oral tradition. The first involves arguments people have about the minutiae of social life. I call the second the literal interpretation of reality. It seems to suggest that certain persons, especially eye witnesses, possess specialized knowledge of specific past events.

Alasdair MacIntyre (1981, 207) writes that living traditions like those found in Lodge Bay are historically extended arguments about the past. Lodge Bay folk are consumed with the details of oral tradition. Emphasis is on *the* facts when listening to people narrate and argue about stories. I often witnessed such arguments during indirect interviewing, when several adults were present. I would ask a question, and one person would begin an answer, only to be "corrected" by another, eventually exploding into a collage of subtly conflicting answers, sometimes leading nowhere. Informants would shout at each other about whether Uncle Joe caught nine or ten quintals of fish, or whether 1963, 1964, or 1967 was the winter with little snow. Like Faris (1972, 149), who observed similar spats in Cat Harbour, Newfoundland, I occasionally felt uncomfortable during these manifestly serious arguments, particularly before I realized that unspoken rules protected all. Faris explains that argumentation must be verbal and controlled: real anger, physical violence, and lies are an affront to the moral community (ibid.).

How are these arguments about the past to be interpreted? There appears to be a sociopolitical dimension to bickering over minutiae, and in this sense knowledge comprising such details actually constitutes an important political resource. Combatants draw upon their existing prestige, their rhetorical skills, and upon their reservoir of "facts." Hence, these confrontations constitute political exchanges insofar as competing individuals attempt to convince an audience about the veracity of their version of reality (Balandier 1970, 35). Arguments about tradition affect the political standing of individuals, as they vie with others to have their version of reality accepted. But the small scale and intimacy of Lodge Bay also means that the opinions of individuals are broadcast and evaluated secondhand through the medium of gossip. A person's reputation may be damaged when others learn that he or she has said something about one thing or another.

The sham arguments about the past I observed closely resemble (except in name) the Newfoundland *cuffers* Faris (1972, 148–149) describes and Sider (1986) analyzes. Cuffers are both antagonistic and intimate lies (insofar as precise details may be inaccurate) about the past, told at "the boundary between the known and the forgotten" (Sider p. 162). Cuffers recreate village history and introduce it to present social relations, expressing the contradictory social tensions that united and divided Newfoundland villages (Sider 1986).

J. Wylie's (1982) study of the social construction of reality among Black Creoles of Casse (Dominica) sheds comparative light on the arguments I heard about Lodge Bay history. For the Creoles, reality is "shiftingly construed, often through argument, as a matter of received opinion, or else it is founded distantly in the antithetical world of white men's ways and God's word" (Wylie 1982, 439). Even Wylie's most reliable informants presented him with bundles of hopelessly confused and unrelated "facts." Like Lodge Bay, genealogical time in Casse only extends back three generations, meaning that history ("a collectively maintained description of the past" p. 446), scarcely exists. Consequently, the past is continually reinvented, through the highly personal interaction of people. As in Lodge Bay, these arguments also evaluate the reputations of disputants, meaning that the outcome, reality itself, may be a temporary coalition between competing personal reputations. One example Wylie provides, the question of whether Dominica is larger or smaller than Guadeloupe, is strikingly similar to the kinds of arguments I witnessed in Labrador.

I call the second, and related, theme in Lodge Bay oral tradition the literal interpretation of reality. During fieldwork in Port Hope Simpson, Labrador, Southard (personal communication, 1982) also observed the literal interpretation of reality. Essentially, certain lore, including some commonly heard stories, is held to be sufficiently complex that only certain persons really knew about it. The synthetic character of the context—with anthropologist poised to codify oral tradition—must be kept in mind (Narváez, personal communication 1994). In such cases and perhaps consequently, people often passed the buck, suggesting that I go ask Uncle John or Aunt Jane about *that*. If the precise details of a story could not be recalled or successfully negotiated through argumentation, then it was better not to tell it at all, lest "we might be telling you a lie." As with religious texts in the hands of literalists, there could be only one true interpretation.

The literal interpretation of reality created some methodological difficulties. In a few cases informants withheld information, apparently thinking (incorrectly) that I would reveal their name in association with a particular version of a story. One day during my second month in the community, for example, I was talking to Gus (a very reliable, knowledgeable, and frequent informant) about historic merchants once operating in the area. Our conversation drifted to a man named Kennelly, who operated a store at Wall's Island early in this century. I mentioned that I had learned about Kennelly's barrens (near Lodge Bay) from another person, whose identity I did not reveal. I then asked Gus if there was any relationship between the merchant Kennelly and the similarly named barrens. He became apprehensive and began wondering aloud if I might use his name as the source of this information. Though I reassured him that I would not, he would offer little more information on the topic. Similarly, this fear of association with specific versions of oral tradition posed another methodological problem: few people permitted use of a tape recorder. Informants usually greeted my requests to tape an interview with "get that thing away" or "shut that off."

The beliefs and practices just discussed are remarkable for their persistence and for the close relationship they expose between people and the environment. The Kerrymen legend, for example, not only fosters social control but also expresses contemporary respect for ancient land use. Lodge Bay oral tradition, the gossip by which people define and portray themselves, is remarkable in its concentration on detail and the local belief that some stories are best told by certain persons.

Chapter 6

Persistence, Change, and Future

The years since 1979 have seen some persistence and many changes in the lives of Lodge Bay folk. The patterns of pronunciation and speech, previously mentioned in relation to Reverend Browne's visit to Cape Charles, persist. One side of a conversation in 1992, 1979, or (I suspect) a hundred years ago, continues to sound like: "Yes maid. . . . Yes, indeed he do. . . . Yes, my dear. . . . Oh he's smart. . . . Yes, for sure." Likewise, in 1992 I heard versions of many of the beliefs and traditions presented in chapter 5. Other examples of persistence were obvious during my return to the community in May and June of 1992.

Lodge Bay people maintain their ardent sense of community consciousness, expressed through many of the same customs, institutions, and groups that I observed in 1979. There is still a nightly schedule of activities and times at the hall, though some complain about certain people leaving too soon after soup is served, thus missing (or perhaps avoiding) the fund-raising activities. There were two such times during my short 1992 visit. The first of these was a card game attended by twenty-eight people; $252 was raised to benefit the Janeway Children's Hospital in distant St. John's, Newfoundland. The second, occurring only six nights later, was a soup supper to benefit the Orange Lodge. Some fifty to sixty people attended, coming from as far north as St. Lewis; each paid $3 a plate, and then later purchased tickets drawn on locally crafted items; the event raised $800. A final expression of continuity is illustrated by the seven-year-long construction of an Anglican church in Lodge Bay, built with volunteer labor, and consecrated on 24 March 1992. Tom pointed proudly to the church to illustrate how cooperation between Lodge Bay folk persists and confidently predicted the community's population would increase.

Many of the changes since 1979 are difficult to separate from broader changes occurring in the province, the nation, and the world. Lodge Bay has become less isolated from the outside world, and more vulnerable to exogenous influences.

During the years preceding the cod moratorium that began in 1992, there were several attempts to diversify a declining fishery. For a couple of years beginning in the early 1980s, Earle Freighting Service (Battle Harbour merchants) encouraged Cape Charles fishers to produce so-called white naped fish, a process involving removal of the black nape membrane covering the interior of eviscerated codfish. A couple of years later, the Labrador Fishermen's Union Shrimp Company purchased salt cod at Cape Charles, followed around 1986, by H. B. Dawe (of Cupids, Newfoundland). Representative of the increased role of women in the wage economy during the 1980s, Dawes employed Cape Charles women to split and salt fish, producing earnings and increasing the number of UI recipients per household.

Dawes's hiring of women in the late 1980s to split and salt the cod that their brothers, husbands, or sons were catching exemplifies the extraordinary growth in the significance of unemployment insurance (UI) benefits in the local economy. Whereas few women drew UI in 1979, many did by 1992, meaning two or more householders were drawing benefits during winter. Moreover, the relative importance of income derived from fish and from UI has changed dramatically. A Mary's Harbour man with considerable knowledge of the fishery told me that whereas fishing once comprised about 60 percent of a fisher's income, and UI about 40 percent, the ratio is now reversed. The explanation of this, as I understand it, involves a reinterpretation (likely by Revenue Canada) of what constitutes an insurable week (or stamp).

During the late 1980s (locals claimed around 1987 or 1988), Cape Charles fishers (and those throughout the region) began selling portions of their dwindling fish catches to different buyers, accumulating more UI stamps with fewer fish. Significantly, the change here appears to be a reinterpretation of an insurable week, redefining it as a sale of fish, irrespective of quantity. In one of few explanations of what constitutes an insurable week (during the mid-1980s), Maura Hanrahan notes that a fisher "cannot obtain a stamp unless he or she has earned over $92" in weekly fish sales (1988, 10). By 1992, however, an insurable week appears to have been any sale of fish. Thus, locals told me how a fisher catching five salmon was better off selling each salmon to five different buyers, accruing five UI stamps, each with a weekly benefit value of $138. One fisher told me how he once lacked a salmon necessary to qualify for a stamp and "had to get the lend 'o one." His son interjected with the story of a salmon fisher who sold salmon to one buyer, bought it back, and then sold it to another, again to obtain insurable weeks (stamps).

Again, the same principle—more UI stamps for fewer fish—applies to the cod fishery. In 1979, fishers earned one stamp for every six quintals (672 pounds) of salt cod sold. By 1992, the amount of fish needed had lessened, though local versions of amounts necessary differed. One man told me that now a crew of four fishers selling one plastic *totebox* (equal to one-half quintal of cod) full of raw fish, head on and gutted, each earned one stamp while another man claimed the sale of any amount of fresh cod qualified for a stamp. All agreed that selling cod to multiple buyers accumulated more stamps, and in the years directly preceding the moratorium, stamps had increasingly become the goal of the fishery. Selling cod fresh, head on and gutted, as opposed to salt bulk (as in 1979), meant that others in the community (sometimes the fishers themselves, working afternoon shifts, but more commonly their wives or children) were employed to split and salt the cod, thus earning wages and accumulating UI stamps. In short, between 1979 and the fishery moratorium, the interpretation of an insurable week changed, and the economy became ever more dependent on UI. More family members qualified for UI even though less fish was produced.

Also, a new development unrelated except in its timing—the 1980s—people began using Citizen's Band (CB) radios at Cape Charles. The exorbitant cost of telephones prompted every house hold to buy a CB, using them to chat between houses (thus reducing visiting), to call the kids home for the midday meal, and to gossip. The CB network stretched from Henley Harbour north to Square Islands (see map 2). People used CB's to talk with boats at sea and credit the technology with saving the lives of Lodge Bay men aboard the floundering longliner *Stacey Renee*. Fishers initially used CB radios to exchange information about the availability of fish but stopped when distant boats converged too quickly on scarce grounds (compare, e.g., Andersen 1972). Peter told me that during the years just prior to the moratorium, "when you don't hear 'em on the CB, then you know they're gettin' some fish."

The End of the Cod Fishery

As noted in chapter 2, Newfoundland's entry into the Canadian federation carried a costly price tag. The 1948 Terms of Union placed the new province under the British North America Act (1867), which surrendered jurisdiction of the offshore, and with it, the cod fishery, the raison d'etre of many small communities like Lodge Bay. Canada benefited substantially, using its control of Newfoundland's rich fishing grounds as an ace to be dealt in its international poker game with European fishing nations. Sadly, Ottawa squandered its jurisdiction of the offshore fishery, meaning that Lodge Bay Settlers, like fishers throughout the new province (most of whom, ironically, supported confederation) enjoyed short-term universal benefits for a very high price: the cod fishery.

The primary change throughout most of Atlantic Canada has been the collapse of the ground fishery—an ecological and social crisis of extraordinary proportions. It is now illegal for Cape Charles fishers to catch cod, even for domestic consumption. Indications of problems with codfish stocks were evident during the 1970s and 1980s, causing the federal Department of Fisheries and Oceans occasionally to reduce the quotas that fishers could catch within the many zones partitioning the oceans off Newfoundland and Labrador; note that Cape Charles is just south of Northwest Atlantic Fisheries Organization division 2J and thus was not included in the 1992 Moratorium). At Black Tickle, Labrador, roughly 140 kilometers north of Cape Charles, the decline of codfish was especially obvious. During the two decades preceding 1990, transient fishers from Newfoundland, Labrador, and the Quebec North Shore swarmed to the once bounteous waters around Black Tickle each summer, overwhelming local fishers and annually catching millions of kilograms. During the summer of 1991 not a single cod was taken.

Throughout Newfoundland and Labrador, declining catches of increasingly smaller codfish led to repeated calls for its closing, especially from those within the fishery. During a speech in February 1990, for example, President of the Fishermen's Union (FFAW/CAW) Richard Cashin warned that the "entire fishing industry faces a crisis of unprecedented proportions, the magnitude of which is not yet understood by either level of government" (Cashin 1990, 6). Government heard similar warnings from commissions chaired by Leslie Harris (1989) and E. B. Dunne (1990) but dragged its heels, perhaps (and understandably) fearing the worst. Meanwhile bureaucrats and politicians busied themselves as if rearranging the deck chairs on the Titanic.

During my visit to Lodge Bay in May and June of 1992, fishers declared that closing the cod fishery was necessary. Like their counterparts throughout Atlantic Canada, and elsewhere in the North Atlantic (see Jentoft 1993), they blamed declining cod stocks on offshore draggers using increasingly lethal technologies. The fish were, as one man put it, "all dragged away."

In 1992, Lodge Bay fishers worried that if the salmon fishery were also closed, they would have "nothing to look forward to." The ancient and highly meaningful seasonal rhythm of life would be severed. Their worry about salmon was well founded. Dwindling salmon stocks and effective international lobbying by recreational salmon anglers led to a federal buy-back (theoretically to last for five years) of commercial salmon licenses in Newfoundland (and voluntarily, in Labrador), just as had occurred in parts of the Canadian Maritimes. By the 31 December 1992 deadline, 89 percent of Newfoundland commercial salmon fishers had sold their licenses back to the federal government (Cleary 1993). By 1994, the 219 fishers on the Labrador coast still holding licenses (including some at Cape Charles) were under new pressures to retire their licenses (*Evening Telegram*, 13 May 1994, 4).

In July 1992 the Canadian government finally announced a moratorium on fishing for "northern cod," shutting down the most important part of Newfoundland's once vital cod fishery. Government paid fishers and plant workers not to work (a subsidy similar to those paid to prairie farmers not to farm), initially leaving around 20,000 jobless. The first reaction from fishers was mixed, ranging from occasional defiant threats of noncompliance to more common, though reluctant, acceptance. The federal government refined the moratorium compensation package, the so-called Northern Cod Adjustment and Recovery Program (NCARP) in August 1992 and broadened eligibility to it.

The moratorium was intended to last two years but by 1993, ground fish stocks off much of Canada's Atlantic coast had declined further, leading to predictions that the fishery might not reopen until the end of the century. By late 1993, the area covered by the moratorium was expanded to include much of Atlantic Canada, affecting in total some 30,000 fishers and plant workers. This extension included the Gulf of St. Lawrence stocks and thus, for the first time, outlawed codfishing from Cape Charles south to the Quebec North Shore. Following this inclusion of the Gulf Stocks came a five-year extension of the financial compensation package, renamed The Atlantic Groundfish Strategy (TAGS). This plan aims to trim the numbers of fishers by reducing monthly compensation and to tie eligibility to retraining inside and outside the fishery. Yet even without the fishery, cod stocks continue to drop. A 1994 federal scientific report estimated northern cod stocks to be only 3 percent of the 1990 total (Cox 1994). All now realize that the social fishery as I observed in 1979 and described in chapter 3 is dead and that any future fishery will be leaner and more professional.

The cod ban hangs over Newfoundland and Labrador like the pall of a coffin. Cape Charles and other fishers are now extremely pessimistic about the future and in this sense the cod ban provides a model from which people now drearily predict the ruination of other species. The fishery crises has become a national issue, with many Canadian editorialists blaming idle fishers and with the federal government attempting to curb foreign overfishing just outside Canada's 200 mile limit, while pressing its case before various international fora. It is an understatement to say that the moratorium has fundamentally distressed Newfoundland society. Unemployed fishers and plant workers are rightly bitter because (while partly to blame) they had predicted such a collapse for many years and now are its victims. Yet outright rebellion is obviated by the ironic fact that some former fishers and plant workers are economically better off on the compensation package than during the final years of the fishery.

But how long will Canadians fund moratoria compensation? Throughout Newfoundland and Labrador, many doubt that the cod fishery will ever return and concede that even if it does, it will never employ as many as it once did.

Two questions are current in Newfoundland and Labrador: why did fish stocks disappear, and what will become of the people and communities long dependent on fishing? The only consensus to these questions is uncertainty. Leaving aside the difficult question of community futures for a moment, one can cite two common explanations for the collapse of the fishery. Fishers cite economic pressures, primarily overfishing; scientists blame natural forces, primarily cold water. The future may someday show a complex blend of these or perhaps other causes.

Another way of talking about the fishery crisis involves changes to the commons, the once rich oceans off Labrador. These changes concern rights to the commons, that is, who can fish and where. Even more immediately are the tragic consequences of Canadian fisheries mismanagement—the empty commons. My use of the commons to discuss the fishery crisis follows a growing number of studies related to the land (Hardin 1968; Behar 1991) and sea (Brox 1990; Jentoft 1993; McCay and Acheson 1987; Matthews 1993). Following Garret Hardin's (1968) seminal essay, these and other studies of the commons underscore the importance of enclosure, the denial of public access to commonly held property, by fence or by law, transforming public resources into private capital. The enclosure off Cape Charles has occurred increasingly since confederation. The state monopolized control of licensing policies, quotas, and seasons. The consequences of Canadian fisheries mismanagement now leave the commons off Cape Charles devoid of cod and, increasingly, of salmon. Moreover, use of the commons under the new crab fishery described below is inimical to that of the customary family-based cod fishery. The crab fishery operates as a corporate enterprise. Access to the commons is strictly regulated through licensing and economic arguments such as labor requirements, boat size, crab pots, and other technologies. In short, the marine commons off Cape Charles are now empty of species once harvested by individual families. Today, Lodge Bay people exploit an increasingly closed commons as wage laborers, following a script drafted by distant bureaucrats and economic exigencies.

The New Economy?

As I talked about economic change with a Lodge Bay couple around their kitchen table one May 1992 night, we were suddenly joined by Joe, their adult son, who interrupted our discussion in midsentence. Emphasizing the community's limited economic potential, Joe looked me in the eye and allowed (with a mixture of humor and insight) that "we all can't be professors!"

Even before the moratorium, the provincial government sought alternatives to the cod fishery and increasingly favored three: tourism, aquaculture, and high-tech industries. Improving the provincial economy will not be easy: Labrador, and indeed all Newfoundland, has a harsh natural setting and a finite number of economic alternatives to its traditional industries.

The main tourist development near Lodge Bay involves restoration of historic Battle Harbour, once capital of the Labrador cod fishery. In 1991, after a couple of years of planning—much of it spearheaded by the Battle Harbour Area Development Association—restoration of Battle Harbour began, under supervision of a nonprofit historic trust composed of business people. The Atlantic Canada Opportunities Agency (ACOA), the Canada Employment and Immigration Commission (CEIC), and the Labrador Rural Development Agreement provided government funding for the project. The plan is reviviscent: to attract tourists to a restored fishing center where former fishers will reenact the salt cod fishery. The concept has some merit, especially given the proximity of three other tourist attractions—the Norse site at L'Anse au Meadows, the Maritime Archaic site at Port au Choix, and the Basque whaling site at Red Bay. Certainly local people from Lodge Bay, Mary's Harbour, and St. Lewis—at least twenty each summer since 1991—welcome the restoration jobs. Yet the locals I interviewed in 1992 emphasized that the success of the project depends entirely on extension of the road from Red Bay north at least to Mary's Harbour, and perhaps beyond, to Goose Bay. Such a road, approximately 475 kilometers in length (from Red Bay to Goose Bay), is estimated to cost more than $2,222 million (Fiander-Good Associates 1993). Whether such a road is built remains to be seen. But even if it is built and if it brings the tourists, two points seem inescapable. Tourism can never replace former labor-intensive economies such as the fishery, and roads are two way: they may bring tourists in, but they also provide Settlers an easy way out.

Thus far, there has been little discussion of high-tech industries for southeastern Labrador communities. And aquaculture, the provincial government's second alternative to fishing, is inhibited by the subarctic waters off Cape Charles. However, a study by the Newlantic Group (1990) and other data show that the snow crab fishery is a promising alternative to the cod fishery. During the 1980s, the Labrador Fishermen's Union Shrimp Company purchased the fish plants at Mary's Harbour and Cartwright, converting them to process snow crab.* Crab production and processing began at Mary's Harbour in 1985, but most Lodge Bay people did not begin working there until 1990. Six crab licenses have been issued to local fishers, who ordinarily lease vessels from Newfoundland and fish in crews of five (including skipper). Moreover, the tedious extraction of crab meat employs most of the labor force available at Mary's Harbour, Lodge Bay, and other communities. Earnings are excellent during the short (ten to fifteen-week) season, and although there are risks associated with the fishery, notably asthma among plant workers, the outlook is promising.

Lodge Bay people have benefitted economically from the new economy that has emerged since about 1990. In recent years some people have helped build a bridge across the St. Charles River, and

---

* The Labrador Fishermen's Union Shrimp Company Limited was formed in 1979 (albeit with a different name) during intense competition over federal allocation of three shrimp licenses to Labrador. With strong and controversial backing from the Newfoundland Fishermen Food and Allied Workers Union (now NFFAW/CAW), the Union Shrimp Company eventually won one of these lucrative licenses, underwriting expansion into other fisheries, including crab.

Crab plant workers at Mary's Harbour plant, 1994. (Photograph by Barbara Neis)

others have worked on the Development Association's construction of a community fishing stage at Indian Cove. Nowadays, some Lodge Bay people work at the restoration of historic Battle Harbour and others work in the snow crab fishery in Mary's Harbour.

Yet the new economy fragments family and community life. It separates families for varying periods of time, some members working in one place, others in another. Some, especially older people, divide their summers between Lodge Bay and an increasingly abandoned Cape Charles. During the summer of 1991, nine Lodge Bay people worked at the Mary's Harbour crab plant while eight men worked restoring Battle Harbour. In the representative case of one Lodge Bay family during that summer, the mother and a son worked for one week at Cape Charles and then nine weeks (August to October) at the crab plant in Mary's Harbour; an adult daughter worked as a bar maid at the Beagle Lounge in Mary's Harbour (living most of the time with her brother who now resides there permanently) while the father and another son fished and commercially smoked salmon at Cape Charles. By contrast, during the summers of 1979 and 1980 all members of this family summered at Cape Charles; the father and two oldest sons formed one of the community's ten fishing crews while the mother and daughter provided essential support. Thus, not only does the new economy remove the need for seasonal transhumance—the economic soul of southeastern Labrador—it shatters the corporate family.

The consequences of these changes, though as yet more apparent in larger southeastern Labrador communities, include increased alcohol consumption, youth alienation, and marital discord. The domestic differences between 1979 and the present are striking. Then, children played ingenuous games around the stages and pathways of Cape Charles, within a stone's throw of the security of kith and hearth. Now children remain in Lodge Bay or in temporary accommodations in Mary's Harbour, watching videos and consuming junk food while their mother and/or father works a shift at the crab plant.

Wages from the crab plant or from Battle Harbour restoration work enable soaring patterns of consumption. Several families have constructed new and larger homes in Lodge Bay, looking more like those one might see in an Atlanta or Toronto subdivision. Finished materials such as gypsum board and countertops must be imported though local men still cut and mill much of the rough timber required. Sawmilling occurs on one of eight (up from five in 1979) sawmills in Lodge Bay. One of these is a new, portable, chainsaw-driven sawmill, which reportedly cuts boards so cleanly that they do not require planing.

The pace of Lodge Bay life has also accelerated. Many people now own trucks or other vehicles. Few walk any distance. The gravel road around Lodge Bay and north to Mary's Harbour is seldom idle, particularly since completion of the bridge across the St. Charles River. Although some lament the loss of trees or privacy resulting from the widened road around the community or fear the theft of possessions once left without thought around their houses, few would or could go back.

Newfoundland-built fiberglass speedboats have replaced locally made wooden boats. Fiberglass boats are less frequently punctured by floating sea ice and are used during winter and spring, especially by those living in outside southeastern Labrador communities like St. Lewis, Black Tickle, and Williams Harbour (see map 2). Fiberglass boats are lighter, less costly on fuel, and more stable than wooden boats. During winter, larger and ever faster snowmobiles increase mobility. In the winter of 1991, a Lodge Bay man sped the approximately 75 kilometers between Red Bay and Lodge Bay in one hour and twenty minutes. Similar and likely faster records undoubtedly exist between Lodge Bay and other communities.

A Look to the Future

Even for soothsayers, predicting the future is always risky business. Even so, I believe that my demographic data reveal difficulties for the years to come. The data include populations from 1935, 1979, and 1992 and necessitate several qualifications before discussion. First, Newfoundland's astonishingly complete 1935 nominal census was taken at Cape Charles, not Lodge Bay; and thus the sixty people listed represent the majority, but not all, of Lodge Bay's winter population. Of course my February 1979 and May 1992 counts occurred at Lodge Bay. In all three censuses, I have purposefully excluded both the few transients (Newfoundland sharemen, teachers, or anthropologists) from the totals, as I have Lodge Bay people who worked permanently in another community and were themselves not in Lodge Bay or Cape Charles during the count or rarely visited their home community. Finally, some conclusions that I draw from the three censuses apply more generally to the aging population of North America.

What do the three censuses (see figures 1–4) tell us about Lodge Bay/Cape Charles? First, I single out four sex and age cohorts which may for convenience be called children (zero to fourteen); reproducing population (fifteen to thirty-nine); middle-aged (forty- to sixty-four); and aged (sixty-five or more). The percentage of children—the hope of the future—is greater in 1935 and 1979 than in 1992. As well, the population is aging, a conclusion obvious from comparison of the middle-aged and aged cohorts in 1979 and 1992 with that in 1935. Growth of the aged population, from 3.3 percent of the total in 1935 to 12.4 percent in 1992 corresponds with provincial and national percentages.

Cohorts between the children and the aged show a disturbing trend. The proportion of the population of reproducing age (fifteen to thirty-nine) is declining, from just under 50 percent in 1935 to about 40 percent in 1979 and 1992. Moreover, the 1992 figure is misleading, insofar as five young women within the 1992 reproducing age group had returned for the summer from university in May 1992 and will not likely settle in Lodge Bay. These university students comprise about a quarter of the female reproducing cohort. On the male side of the ledger, also from 1992, note how few men there are in the two five-year age cohort (e.g., twenty-five to twenty-nine and thirty-five to thirty-nine), reflecting the exodus of young males from the village.

Over all, there has been a decline in population from 125 in 1979 to 97 in 1992. Troubling and historically unprecedented is male emigration. Traditionally, young men remained with the fishery

Figure 1

1935 Population Pyramid by Age/Sex (Cape Charles)

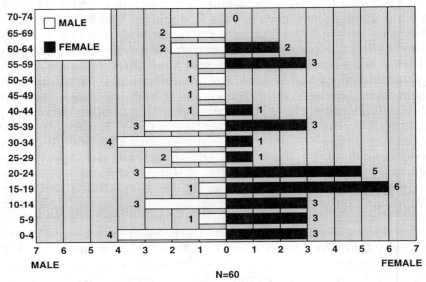

1935 Age/Sex Cohorts by Percentage (Cape Charles)

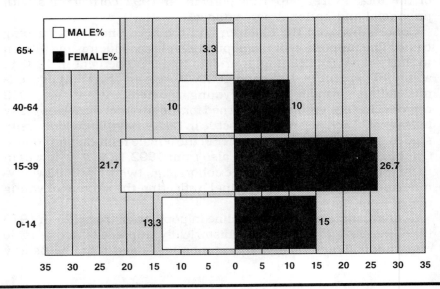

Figure 2

1979 Population Pyramid by Age/Sex (Lodge Bay)

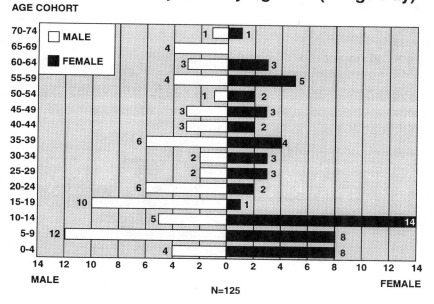

1979 Age/Sex Cohorts by Percentage (Lodge Bay)

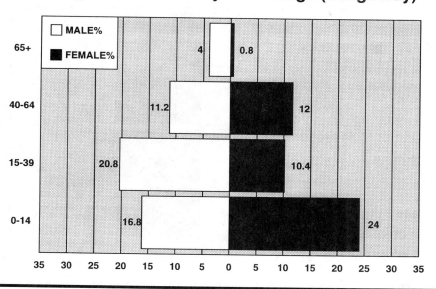

Figure 3

1992 Population Pyramid by Age/Sex (Lodge Bay)

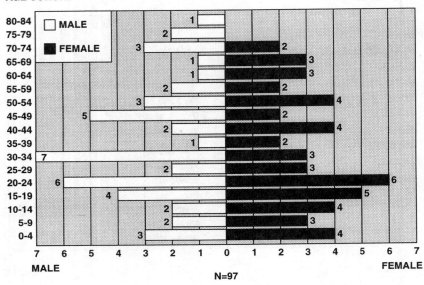

1992 Age/Sex Cohorts by Percentage (Lodge Bay)

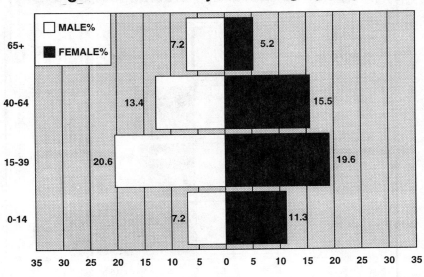

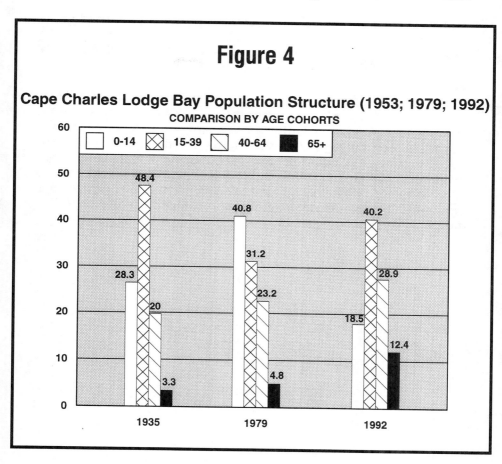

Figure 4

Cape Charles Lodge Bay Population Structure (1953; 1979; 1992)
COMPARISON BY AGE COHORTS

Legend: 0-14 | 15-39 | 40-64 | 65+

1935: 28.3, 48.4, 20, 3.3
1979: 40.8, 31.2, 23.2, 4.8
1992: 18.5, 40.2, 28.9, 12.4

while their sisters moved elsewhere to marry or work. Lodge Bay folk are of two minds about their sons leaving. On the one hand the main cause of emigration—an imperiled fishery—worries everyone, while on the other hand, people reluctantly accept that opportunities are better elsewhere. Mainly young people leave, but some older people might like to. As middle-aged Bob told me, "I'd get out of it if I could but it's too late to start anew." People realize that the future of their community rests with the Mary's Harbour crab fishery. As go crab prices and availability, so goes Lodge Bay (and Mary's Harbour).

Other indications of a shrinking community can be inferred from the local school, educating only half as many students in 1992 as in 1979. Moreover, the entire 1991–92 school year occurred at Lodge Bay, further evidence of the wane of seasonal transhumance.

Older people blame the shrinking enrollment on unmarried youth not having children. However, as I see it, the decisions taken by single youth, many only in their twenties, are a manifestation of new, and unequaled, economic uncertainties overwhelming the community.

The economic forces crashing against the Labrador coast will lead to the slow demise of some communities. With the exception of the crab fishery, which certainly ensures economic security for some in the short term, I doubt that the alternatives described can provide for the present population. I foresee instead the decline of the community by attrition, with the young emigrating and their elders remaining to work in the crab fishery. The years ahead will undoubtedly test the determination and ingenuity of Lodge Bay people.

Appendix 1

Local Terms and Expressions

These are some vernacular terms and expressions I heard and recorded at Lodge Bay/Cape Charles, written here phonetically. My definitions purposefully attempt *not* to rely on existing sources, so as to serve future lexicographers. Existing sources include two brief lexicons published during the early 1930s (Evans 1930; Strong 1931) and the definitive *Dictionary* compiled by Story, Kirwin, and Widdowson (1982).

Alexander. Edible, green, leafy plant that grows by the landwash.

Aunt. Classificatory term of affection and respect given to an older, usually unrelated, female.

Bakeapple. A circumpolar edible berry, elsewhere known as cloudberry; *Rubus chamaeoreus.*

Balk. Hagdown bird.

Bang belly. Plain molasses cake without raisins.

Barkin' nets. Dying nets dark brown.

Barter note. Receipt for sale of products (like seals), often written in a notebook showing value of sale.

Bawn. Cobbled round stones on which codfish are dried.

Berth. Valued location where fish or seal nets are set.

Blackberry fish. Codfish full of a small organism that resembles a blackberry.

Blacky-boy timber. A tree scorched by a forest fire, cut down and used as fuel.

Bladder. A bulbous protrusion on balsam fir trees, containing turpentine; once used as a medicine to stop bleeding (also called turpentine mur).

Blubber. Rotted cod livers.

Bobber. Corked and hooked device once used to retrieve slain migratory waterfowl.

Bog bean.   Green marsh plant; used as a medicine for flu and as an appetite stimulant for those suffering from cancer.

Boggie.   Canvas tent stove.

Boiler.   A large caldron.

Bonds.   Flat or cobbled rocks, purposefully placed together to dry codfish on.

Boot jack.   Used to soften sealskin boots.

Brewis.   Plain, hard bread that is soaked, cooked, and served with codfish.

Bridge.   A porch or deck.

Broken couple roof.   A gambrel or barn-styled roof once common in Lodge Bay and Cape Charles (also called bell roofs).

Brook.   Well or other source of potable water.

Bulk.   Layered, wet, salted codfish.

Bulldog Fish.   Blunt-nosed codfish. It was once said that you would get one every 100 quintals. Old men would say, "bye', that's a good sign . . . there's another load fur [for] us."

Bullybagger.   An evil, devilish creature.

Byhalder.   Threatening figure, similar to Bullybagger.

Byline.   A vertical rope running from the mainline of a longline to surface buoys.

Caplin skul fish.   Same as trap fish.

Chimley.   Stove chimney.

Coachbox.   A rectangular bottomless box tied on top of a komatik used to carry passengers and, sometimes, junked firewood.

Cod knocker.   A metal device once used to scare cod into a cod seine.

Cod trap.   Netted boxes set in the ocean close to land, with an opening through which cod swim and become entrapped.

Cooked dinner.   A large meal which includes cooked meats, vegetables, and various steamed puddings.

Copying.   Children imitating adult behavior.

Cosh.   A brook or a stream.

Cossack.   A locally made white canvas hooded jacket, popular before Confederation.

Couldnins'.   Leftover food; food that you could not eat yesterday.

Crooked timbers.   Interior ribbing of boat.

Cross (fox).   A gray-colored fox with a dark cross marking on its back.

Cuddy.   Enclosed storage space at bow of fishing boat.

Cuffer.   Newfoundland term for oral history.

Cutch.   Bark used to dye nets dark brown.

Dabbers.   The hook portion plus connecting saidline on cod longline.

Damper dog.   Bread dough cooked on top of stove.

Daybed.   A couch, often sloped, for reclining on.

Deep net.   A seal net set in shoal (shallow) water. Used "outside" (on outer coast). It has a 35 cm mesh, is fifteen meshes deep, and is shorter in length than a shoal net.

Deep water fish.   Large codfish caught on longline in autumn, often with little in its stomach.

Dirty water. Sea water with considerable slub, which makes nets more visible to fish; locally believed to vary in extent with water temperatures.

Douser. Similar to cod knocker, containing rings that rattle.

Draw up. To dry. People rationalize painting the exterior of wooden boats white so that they will not dry out and leak as would darker colors (like green) when exposed to the sun, when a boat is overturned on land.

Droke. An open area surrounded by a few trees.

Duff. A steamed pudding containing raisins, bakeapples, or blueberries.

Faggot. A circular pile of green salt fish.

Fairy head(ed). Disoriented after an encounter with the fairies.

Fish store. A building for storing salted codfish and other fishing possessions.

Flake. A wooden platform on which codfish are dried.

Flanker. A hot spark from a stove or stove pipe.

Foggidies. Wood shavings used as matches to light a pipe or cigarette.

Gam bird. A migratory game bird, such as eider duck.

Gandi. Identical to damper dogs, except cooked in a frying pan.

Gathering. A pus-filled skin boil.

Gaze. A blind, usually made of snow, behind which hunters hunt ducks.

Ghost net. Unmoored or derelict net, particularly gill nets, which continue to kill fish.

Gib. The entrails and gills of herring.

Gill net. A monofilament fishing net which ensnares fish by the gills, causing them to suffocate.

Green fish. Salted damp codfish, otherwise known as a salt bulk cod.

Greens. Immature, domesticated locally grown cabbage or turnip tops, or wild Alexander.

Ground. A location where fish or fur-bearing animals are likely to be found.

Ground juniper. A low coniferous bush, the branches of which were boiled and used as a cold remedy.

Grump. A vertical wharf post at the end of a wharf.

Hag, the hag, or **ol' hag.** A nightmare in which the dreamer believes he/she is awake and grabbed in the stomach by an old woman.

Hand barrel. A box supported and carried by two long handles. Used for carrying items over rough terrain.

Harbor rule. Locally agreed upon use of the commons.

Hard. Indomitable, as in a hard man.

Header. A crew member who rips off codfish heads.

Heading palm. Knitted covering for palm of hand, used when heading codfish.

Herring fish. Large codfish containing herring in stomachs.

Ice needles. Vertical slivers of ice which freeze over night on spring river ice.

In collar. Said to be a Newfoundland term to describe stationer fisher workers whose summer wages were paid at the end of the summer's fishing voyage.

Injun tea. A small bushlike plant, also called Labrador tea.

Janneys. Masked, yuletide visitors.

Jigger. Molded lead fishing lures with two hooks, used to attract and catch codfish.

Jigging. A form of handline fishing in which a jigger is pulled up and down to catch fish.

Jobbies. Shavings used to light fire or pipe.

Jowler. Codfish, larger than a deep water fish, caught on longline in autumn. So named because neck must be partially severed with knife before heading.

Juniper. Term for the larch tree; *Larix laricina.*

Junks. Firewood sawed to stove length.

Keep. To maintain or respect a practice, as in keeping Sunday.

Kerrymen. Unknown ancestral population.

Komatik. An Inuit word for sled or sledge that is pulled by dog or snowmobile traction.

Kyanne. The real thing is said to be "the real kyanne."

Lady's Twist. An old brand of chewing tobacco.

Landwash. The seashore.

Lapstrake. A small wooden boat in which the exterior planking is overlapped like clapboard on a house.

'laska salmon. Late summer salmon, pale in color.

Lee shore fish. Salmon are said to be a lee shore fish, most plentiful when the wind blows them on shore. At Cape Charles, an easterly wind, blowing toward the shore, is therefore considered the best wind direction in which to catch salmon.

Linnet. Rough twine used to make nets.

Longline. A line running along the ocean with baited hooks. Often called a trawl.

Lunch. A light meal eaten between main meals.

Lund. A location that is sheltered from the wind.

Mainline. A fishing line set on the ocean floor from which saidlines originate.

Make. To sun dry codfish.

Mall dow. Hairlike, greenish grey moss growing on spruce or fir trees.

Mccarry chick. A small grey bird having a strong, oily, and repugnant odorous liquid coming from its nose, possibly as a defensive mechanism. It comes out in the night or in fog and breeds on edge of cliffs.

Mesh. Marsh or bog.

Moon fallin' back. New moon.

Motorboat. An open wooden boat about 9 meters long with an inboard engine. Also called a trapboat.

Mother Wall. A Cape Charles threatening figure.

Muzzle loader. An archaic single-shot rifle.

Nish. Tender meat.

Not too easy. A complimentary appraisal of a person with considerable talents or a comment passed about a person who has just accomplished an extraordinary act.

Oilskins. Waterproof, protective clothing, now made of nylon or rubber.

Old people. The ancestors.

On halves. Division of products whereby the owner of essential technology receives one half and the producer of raw material the other half.

On the hook. Aggravated or frustrated when something goes unexpectedly wrong.

Paddle. Boat oar.

Pinnacle hole. A hole through the sea ice over a rock caused by tidal action; in spring, garbage is thrown into it.

Pip. The entrails and air sack of herring.

Plem. A description of how boat planks swell and tighten once a boat puts from land in to water.

Pond trout. A small sea-run brook trout, caught in nets in salt water.

Prong. A two-pronged pitch fork formerly used to move codfish.

Queer things. Unexplainable phenomena, such as mysterious lights.

Quintal. An archaic unit of measurement for 112 pounds, or 50.8 kilograms, of formerly dried, now green or salt bulk, codfish.

Raken' stems. Used to describe the angle of the keel to the stem or bow of a boat, especially a speedboat.

Rampsing. Jocular jousting, sometimes leading to a fight.

Randy. Child's play, such as sliding.

Rind. Tree bark used to cover buildings (houses, stages).

Rodney. A small, round-bottom, wooden rowboat.

Room. Fishing structures located at the water's edge, including stages, stores, and flakes.

Saidline. Short fishing line with baited hook, running along the mainline of a cod longline, spaced about one meter from the next.

Sampson. A mangy red fox with shedding fur; possibly diseased (also called Woods Ranger).

Saw log. A large log milled for boards.

Scattered. A few, some.

Scoff. A good-sized meal, sometimes, though not necessarily, of stolen food.

Sculling hole. Hole in stern of small boat through which sculling oar is placed for moving boat through the water.

Sculling oar. One large oar used to skull (single paddle) a boat; once common along the coast.

Scunning. Putting the bottom on a cod trap.

Shading knife. A long-bladed, wood-handled knife formerly used to scrape fat off bay sealskins.

Shelly. Wood (usually old) which peels or splinters into small strips.

Shoal crab. A shrew which eats snared rabbits (sometimes called beal or bill mouse).

Shoal net. A seal net, approximately 40 fathoms long. Used in bays, set on the bottom; has a 21 cm mesh and is ten to twelve meshes deep.

Shoryur. Old shore drake (duck).

Skidoo. A snowmobile, a motorized vehicle for snow travel.

Skipper. Leader and often boat owner of a fishing crew; term of respect for older man.

Slop. Codfish which has been dried only three days.

Slub. Green, viscous plankton which adheres to fish nets; also called dirty water.

Smutty harp. Dark skinned old harp seal; skins used for dog team traces.

Snoberly crouches. Pieces of wood used in boat building to keep the sides of a boat apart once the molds have been taken out.

Solid knee. Angled interior braces of a boat to which the sides are nailed.

Spawning fish. Fish pregnant with roe; large fish.

Split longer ("Lunger"). A log split in two; used in wharf and staging construction.

Splits. Kindling for starting fires.

Spring herring. Herring accidentally caught in cod trap.

Spruce beer. A medicinal tonic made of spruce or juniper boughs, later used as an alcoholic beverage.

Stage. Log scaffolding over saltwater, often supporting flakes, fish stores, and other fishing properties.

Stall. A tubular, knitted, yarn finger protector used when jigging cod.

Stamp. An insurable week under the Canadian Unemployment Insurance system.

Stanchion. A corner post on rafts once used to haul wood out of the bay.

Stem. Bow or front of a boat.

Stick. Log used for construction or fuel.

Struck fish. Codfish which has laid in bulk for at least 21 days and, therefore, can be sun dried or sold for commercial drying.

Stumpbox. A box tied atop a komatik to hold cut wood (shorter than a coachbox).

Sun hound. A ring around the sun, a harbinger of western wind.

Switch. Short stick used to beat and clean slub from nets.

Tell-tale diver. A shore bird the size of a shell bird but smaller than a loon; part feather, part fur "on its ass"; webbed, three toed; rarely seen at Cape Charles.

Them times. The past.

Those days. The present time.

Tickle. A narrow passage of water between two bodies of land.

Time. A public social event which may be for fund-raising and which may include a supper of donated food, a raffle or lottery of donated items, and/or a dance.

Tippy moon. Quartered moon.

Toast bread. Toasted bread.

Token. An unusual stimulus portending a future event, often death.

Toll pin(s). One or two vertical wooden pegs, used as oar locks for rowing small boats.

Tormented. A description of someone who is bothered, often by pranks.

Totebox. A plastic fish container which holds one-half quintal of codfish.

Trap fish. Small to medium sized codfish feeding on caplin (sometimes called caplin skul fish).

Trawl. Local term used for baited longline.

Tuckabows. Dwarf spruce, common to exposed headlands.

Turpentine. The sap of balsam fir.

Turpentine mur. A bulbous protrusion on balsam fir containing turpentine; once used to heal cuts (also called bladders).

Twine work. Mending of fishing nets.

Ulu. A curvilinear Inuit knife used for scraping fat from seal skins. While older people were uncertain as to the Inuktitut name, they were aware of the knife and used a version of the word ulu.

Uncle. Classificatory term of affection and respect given to an older, usually unrelated, male.

Utta. Dog team command to turn left.

Uuk. Dog team command to turn right.

Vir. Local term for balsam fir tree.

Waterhorses. Piles of green salt fish, concentrated to squeeze out water.

Whit. A circular-shaped rope, attached to the toll pin used for rowing a dory.

Whitten. A tree from which rinds are taken.

Windshook. When water gets into a tree, freezes, and splits the wood.

Woo. Dog team command to stop.

Wood horns. Carved vertical sticks atop a komatik to retain logs.

Woodslide. Heavy sledge to haul wood over snow (sometimes called catamaran).

Winter fish. Small salted codfish used for domestic winter consumption.

Appendix 2

A Twentieth-Century Chronology, 1900–1978

As throughout the book, all persons alive during the 1979 fieldwork period are here given pseudonyms, a point that may well cause some consternation among Labrador readers. Also, as noted in the text, the chronology contains some factual errors, notably the dating of Hatter's Cove hospital. However, such errors are very understandable given how little has been written on the area. Moreover, the strengths of the chronology easily compensate for such errors, as it presents important historical events—the first cigarette smoked, the first thefts at Norman Bay and Henley Harbour, the early use of gill nets, and others.

1909. Bob Rumbolt's (of Mary's Harbour) father purchases his first motorboat engine.

Early 1900s. Stationer Bob Allen dies at Pleasure Harbour, body stored in cave during summer.

Cape Charles people go to Corner Brook for fall herring fishery.

About 1919. Co-op Store operates at Cape Charles, managed by Freeman Dicks, who also had store at Lodge Bay.

11 December 1919. SS *Ethie* runs aground just north of Sally's Cove (Newfoundland), en route from Curling to Battle Harbour.

Early 1920s. Ephrain Pye buys the first motorboat engine at Cape Charles.

1921 to about 1923. A Mr. Tobin operates a pit prop cutting operation in St. Lewis Bay.

About 1927. Amalgamation of two Lodge Bay schools (Up the Brook and former Rabbit Brook schools).

First crystal radio at Battle Harbour.

About 1929.   Large lobster caught in cod trap leader at Henley Harbour;
another caught about 1953.

Injun Cove (Cape Charles) fishermen complain about fish prices
offered by Baine Johnston.

1929.   Corner Brook (Newfoundland) mill begins.

About 1930.   George Allen first buys fresh salmon at Cape Charles, paying
three cents a pound.

Sam Acreman employed by IGA, at Mary's Harbour; Acremans and
Cumbys original Mary's Harbour families.

About 1932–33.   IGA builds hospital at Hatter's Cove, St. Lewis Inlet.

1930s.   Bebe Gardener Stone teaches school at Lodge Bay; people learn
about rafting of wood.

About 1934.   "Dr." Moses Earl visits Cape Charles.

About 1937.   Banikhin opens herring fishery at Cape Charles.

1937.   Coastal boat trip between Carbonear and Battle Harbour costs $3.

1939.   Aladdin lamps replace earlier oil lamps at Cape Charles.

About 1940.   First domesticated house cat at Cape Charles; Joe Pye's
father obtains it from St. Anthony.

1941.   Americans buy land at White Point from Jack Murphy.

1940s.   Admiral Donald MacMillan gets water at Antle's Cove.

1942.   Lew Pye and two other Lodge Bay men go to work in Goose Bay.

Only year of work for Lodge Bay men at White Point.

1944.   Mrs. Even Stone operates Post Office at Henley Harbour.

About 1944.   St. Lewis (Fox Harbour) people cease wintering at River Head
(St. Lewis Inlet).

Jake and Earl Pye work for the Americans at Tessialuk (near Cape
Harrison, Northern Labrador).

Last Hillyard lives at Green Bay.

Joe Pye sees young woman smoking on coastal boat.

Mid-1940s.   Eric Blackwood starts Eastern Provincial Airways (EPA), flies
mail to Labrador.

1946.   Forest fire at Lodge Bay.

Lodge Bay people discover old barrel hoops after '46 fire.

Lodge Bay people stop rafting summer firewood to Cape Charles.

About 1947.   Thirteen Newfoundland welfare recipients work at Port Hope
Simpson. They walked to Lodge Bay to get coastal boat to St. John's.

Twenty-five caribou killed by St. Lewis (Fox Harbour) hunters.

About 1949.   Cigarette smoking begins at Cape Charles.

About 1950.   Lew Pye purchases house and premises from George Pye.

Early 1950s.   Two years Baine Johnston does not sell fishery salt.

About 1950 to early 1970s.   Few rabbits in southeast Labrador; they start
to return about 1972 or 1974.

1952. Jim Pye purchases a room at Carrol's Cove; his brother Reg relocates there in 1950.

1953. Mrs. Tom Stone (Henley Harbour) has first radio telephone at Henley Harbour.

1953 or 1954. Road built between Matthews Cove and Indian Cove.

About 1954. Earle's Freighting Service takes over from Baine Johnston at Battle Harbour.

Fourteen Moose introduced at River Head (St. Lewis Inlet).

Francis Banikhin had herring plant at Matthews Cove.

1955. Hurricane Iona ("Ion") devastates Cape Charles.

About 1955. Cape Charles people stop using wooden "trillings" in wharf construction.

About 1956. Tim Bradley left Indian Cove for Kyre's Cove, Mary's Harbour, and ultimately Lodge Bay.

U.S. Radar Base begins near St. Lewis (Fox Harbour).

1956. Otter Bay people begin wintering at Norman Bay.

Forest fire starts in St. Lewis Inlet and burns toward Port Hope Simpson.

1958 or 1959. Kenneth Pye purchases first snowmobile in Lodge Bay.

About 1959. One of the Bradleys purchases a speedboat.

1960s. Pitt's Arm has four operating sawmills.

About 1960. Lump noted on porcupine rib sections.

Jim Acreman purchases first power toboggan in Mary's Harbour.

Until 1961. Mails flown to Lodge Bay, then taken to Battle Harbour weekly.

About 1961 or 1964. Jerry and Bob Shaw Carnival comes to Cape Charles.

1961. First autobagan purchased.

About 1962. Fishery Products moves out of Henley Harbour.

Last caribou (about 25) killed by Pinsent's Arm hunters.

About 1963 or 1964. St. Lewis (Fox Harbour) fishermen begin drawing for cod trap berths.

About 1964. Battle Harbour "slub" (in nets) problems begin.

Some Cape Charles women begin smoking.

1965 or 1966. Brothers Eric and Herman Pye first use gill nets.

1967. A theft occurs in Norman Bay.

About 1968. Many Battle Harbour people cease wintering there.

About 1969. Dave Hunt and the Griffin family are "starved out" of Camp Island fishery.

1970. Brothers Eric and Herman Pye's cod crew fissions and they each fish on their own.

Pitt's Arm closes.

Until 1970. Lodge Bay people leave Lodge Bay about 20 April for Cape Charles.

1971.   A theft occurs in Henley Harbour.

1973.   Last time there were rats in Cape Charles.

About 1975.   Cape Charles people stop netting harp seals.

Winter of 1976–77.   Provincial government pays subsidies on air freight of perishable foods flown to southeast Labrador.

About 1977.   Northern Labrador Inuit lost and found in St. Michael's Bay.

1977.   Community stage built at Henley Harbour; leased by Central Diaries (Stephenville) for three years.

1978.   Pinsent's Arm men use Canada Works project to build community stage.

References Cited

Abbreviations used:

ADSF Among the Deep Sea Fishers (journal)
MUNFLA Memorial University of Newfoundland Folklore and Language Archive
PC Privy Council (British) Judicial Committee. 1927. In the matter of the boundary between the Dominion of Canada and the colony of Newfoundland in the Labrador peninsula, between the Dominion of Canada of the one part and the colony of Newfoundland of the other. 12 vols. London: W. Clodwes & Sons
TD Them Days (magazine)

Abbott, W. S. 1974. The 'time.' MUNFLA 74-145.

Adams, M. 1971. MUNFLA 71-5/13.

Andersen, R. 1972. Hunt and Deceive: Information Management in Newfoundland Deep-Sea Trawler Fishing. In R. Andersen & C. Wadel, *North Atlantic Fishermen*. Social and Economic Papers, No. 5. St. John's: Institute of Social and Economic Research.

Arensberg, C. M. [1937] 1988. *The Irish Countryman*. Prospect Heights, IL: Waveland Press.

Arensberg, C. M., & S. T. Kimball. 1965. *Culture and Community*. New York: Harcourt, Brace & World.

Auger, R. 1991. *Labrador Inuit and Europeans in the Strait of Belle Isle: From the Written Sources to the Archaeological Evidence*. Quebec: Centre d'études nordiques, University of Laval.

Balandier, G. 1970. *Political Anthropology*. New York: Pantheon.

Baughman, E. W. 1966. *Type and Motif: Index of Folktales of England and North America*. The Netherlands: Mouton.

Beauharnois, C., Marquis de, & G. Hocquart. 1743. Extension of concession, 7 Sept. 1743, to Marsal for 6 years, 1744–1750. *PC* 7(1406): 3663.

———. 1735. Concession, 27 Sept. 1735, of Cap Charles to Sieur Marsal for 6 years, 1735–44. *PC* 7(1405): 3662.

Behar, R. 1991. *The Presence of the Past in a Spanish Village*. Princeton: Princeton University Press.

Bell, C., & H. Newby. 1978. *Community Studies*. London: George Allen & Unwin.

Bellah R., R. Madsen, W. M. Sulivan, A. Swidler, & S. M. Tipton. 1985. *Habits of the Heart: Individualism and Commitment in American Life*. Berkeley: University of California Press.

Berger, J. 1979. *Pig Earth*. London: Writers and Readers.

Brody, H. 1982. *Irishkillane: Change and Decline in the West of Ireland*. London: Jill Norman & Hobhouse.

Browne, P. W. 1909. *Where the Fishers Go: The Story of Labrador*. New York: Cochrane.

Brox, O. 1990. The Common Property Theory: Epistemological Status and Analytical Utility. *Human Organization* 49(3): 227–235.

———. 1968. Resettlement in Newfoundland. In M. L. Skolnick (ed.), *Viewpoints on Communities in Crisis*. Newfoundland Social and Economic Papers, No. 1. St. John's: Institute for Social and Economic Research.

Burdett, H. 1967. MUNFLA. Q 67-121.

Burdett, J. 1979. Some smoker stories. *TD*, vol. 4(4): 5.

Butler, G. R. 1985. Supernatural Folk Belief Expression in a French-Newfoundland Community: A Study of Expressive Form, Communicative Process, and Social Function in L'Anse-a-Canards. Unpublished Ph.D. dissertation, Memorial University of Newfoundland.

Cadigan, S. 1990. Battle Harbour in Transition: Merchants, Fishermen, and the State in the Struggle for Relief in a Labrador Community during the 1930s. *Labour/Le Travail*, 26: 125–150.

Canadian Salt Fish Corporation. 1981. Brief Presented to the Royal Commission to Inquire into the Inshore Fishery of Newfoundland and Labrador.

Cartwright, G. 1792. *A Journal of Transactions and Events during a Residence of Nearly Sixteen Years on the Coast of Labrador*. Newark: Allin and Ridge (3 vols.).

Casey, G. 1967. Light and Suicide House. MUNFLA 67.032: 034.

Cashin, R. 19 February, 1990. Campaign for Survival. Address delivered at Hotel Newfoundland, St. John's, Newfoundland.

Clark, D. B. 1973. The Concept of Community: A Re-examination. *Sociological Review* 21(3): 397–416.

Clark, L. M. 1978. Growing up in Henley Harbour: An interview with Lloyd Stone. MUNFLA 78-327.

Clark, R. 1986. Romancing the Harlequins. In R. Clark (ed.), *Contrary Winds*. St. John's, Newfoundland: Breakwater.

Cleary, R. 4 January, 1993. Fishermen cashing in licences. *Evening Telegram*, St. John's, Newfoundland.

Cohen, A. P. 1985. *The Symbolic Construction of Community*. New York: Tavistock Publications.

Corbett, L. 1976. Teenage life on Battle Harbour Island. MUNFLA 76-214.

Cox, K. 29 June, 1994. Fish on Wane Despite Effort to Save Them. *Globe & Mail*, A4, Toronto, Ontario.

Creighton, H. 1988. *The Best of Helen Creighton*. Hantsport, Nova Scotia: Lancelot Press.

Davis, D. L. 1983. *Blood and Nerves*. Newfoundland Social and Economic Studies, No. 28. St. John's: Institute of Social and Economic Research.

Davis, H. 1967. MUNFLA 67-274.

Davis, J. C. 1977. Grady Whale Factory Smoke and Steam. *TD* 3(2): 4–8.

Duquesne, M., & F. Bigot. 1753. Cancellation of grant to Baune and regrant to Marsal, 24 Sept. 1735, for nine years, 1754–63. *PC* 7(1408): 3667.

Dunne, E. B. 1990. *Report of the Implementation Task Force on Northern Cod*. Ottawa: Fisheries and Oceans Canada.

Dyke, A. P. 1969. Community Inventory of Coastal Labrador. St. John's: Department of Labrador Affairs.

Evening Telegram. 13 May, 1994. Salmon Stocks Shrinking: Licence Buyback May Not Be Enough, 4, St. John's, Newfoundland.

Evans, M. S. 1930. Terms from the Labrador Coast. *American Speech* 6(1): 56–58.

Faris, J. C. 1972. *Cat Harbour: A Newfoundland Fishing Settlement*. Newfoundland Social and Economic Studies, No. 3. St. John's: Institute of Social and Economic Research.

Fiander-Good Associates. 1993. *Trans Labrador Highway: Social and Economic Project Feasibility Analysis Condensed Final Report*. Fredericton, NB.

Ford, A. 1977. If I Seen a Ghost I'd Almost Faint. *TD* 3(2): 33–34.

Fornel, L. 1742. Fornel's report re: Baye des Chateaux and application for authority to explore Baye des Esquimaux, 27 Oct. 1742. *PC* 7(1402): 3656.

Fraser, A. M. 1958. Newfoundland. In *Encyclopedia America*, Canadian edition. Toronto: Americana Corporation of Canada.

Goudie, E. 1973. *Woman of Labrador*. Toronto: Peter Martin Associates.

Grenfell, W. T. 1919. *A Labrador Doctor: The Autobiography of Wilfred Thomason Grenfell*. Boston: Houghton Mifflin.

Gushue, G. 1968. MUNFLA 68-009 F, 152.

Hanrahan, M. 1988. *Living on the Dead*. St. John's: Institute for Social and Economic Research.

Hardin, G. 1968. The Tragedy of the Commons. *Science* 162:1243–1248.

Harris, L. 1989. *Independent Review of the State of the Northern Cod Stock*. Ottawa: Fisheries and Oceans Canada.

Higgins, B., & C. Liska. 4 April, 1989. Labrador Fishery: Latest News Hard to Locate. *The Labradorian*.

Hillary, G. A. 1955. Definitions of community: Areas of agreement. *Rural Sociology* 20: 111–23.

Hiscock, E. (MHA). 1981. Royal Commission on Inshore Fisheries of the Province of Newfoundland and Labrador.

Implementation Task Force on Northern Cod. (E. B. Dunne, Chairman, Director General, Newfoundland Region, Department of Fisheries and Oceans Canada). October 1990. Report.

Jacobs, J. 1967. MUNFLA FSL 67-9/111.

James, C. D. 1971. Reminiscences of My Childhood Experiences of the Labrador Fishery. MUNFLA 71-103.

Jentoft, S. 1993. *Dangling Lines*. Social and Economic Studies, No. 50. St. John's: Institute for Social and Economic Research.

Jones, L. 1944. The Ghosts of New York: An Analytical Study. *Journal of American Folklore* 57: 237–254.

Junek, O. W. 1937. *Isolated communities: A Study of a Labrador Fishing Village*. New York: American Book Company.

Kaufman, H. F. 1959. Toward an interactional conception of community. *Social Forces* 38: 8–17.

Kennedy, J. C. 1982. *Holding the Line: Ethnic Boundaries in a Northern Labrador Community*. Social and Economic Studies, No. 27. St. John's: Institute for Social and Economic Research.

_____. 1988. The Changing Significance of Labrador Settler Ethnicity. *Canadian Ethnic Studies* 20(3): 94–111.

_____. 1995. *People of the Bays and Headlands: Anthropological History and the Fate of Communities in the Unknown Labrador*. Toronto: University of Toronto Press.

Lajonquiere, Marquis de, & F. Bigot. Grant, 1 Nov. 1749. of Cape Charles to Capt. Baune (deBonne) for 9 years, 1750–59. *PC* 7 [1407]: 3665.

Loring, S. 1992. Princes and Princesses of Ragged Fame: Innu Archaeology and Ethnohistory in Labrador. Ph.D. Diss., Department of Anthropology, University of Massachusetts, Amherst.

Lyon, L. 1987. *The Community in Urban Society*. Philadelphia: Temple University Press.

MacIntyre, A. 1981. *After Virtue: A Study in Moral Theory*. Notre Dame, IN: University of Notre Dame Press.

MacKay, F., M. P. Jackson, and V. J. B. Hanley. 1980. Job Creation: Its Impact on Crofting Communities. *Scottish Journal of Sociology* 4(2): 93–103.

Matthews, D. R. 1993. *Controlling Common Property*. Toronto: University of Toronto Press.

McCay, B. J. & J. M. Acheson (eds.) 1987. *The Question of the Commons*. Tucson: University of Arizona Press.

Mesher, R. 1967. MUNFLA Q 67-784.

Montell, W. L. 1975. *Ghosts along the Cumberland*. Knoxville: University of Tennessee Press.

Moss diary. 1832. Remarks at Battle Harbour from 9 Feb. 1832 to 7 Sept. 1932. GN P3/B/3. Provincial Archives of Newfoundland and Labrador.

Narváez, P. 1987. "Newfoundland Berry Pickers 'In the Fairies': The Maintenance of Spatial and Temporal Boundaries through Legendry." *Lore and Language*, 6 (1): 15–49.

Newfoundland. 1986. Royal Commission on Employment and Unemployment (RCEU). *Building on Our Strengths: Final Report of the Royal Commission*. (J. D. House, chairman).

Newlantic Group. 1990. *A Development Plan for a New Crab Resource off the Coast of Labrador.* St. John's: Department of Fisheries and Oceans.

Oliver, V. 1970. MUNFLA FSL 70-23/124.

Ong, W. 1982. *Orality and Literacy.* London: Methuen.

Payne, R. 1964. MUNFLA FSL 64-5/67.

Plaice, E. 1990. *The Native Game.* Social and Economic Studies No. 40. St. John's: Institute for Social and Economic Research.

Pye, J. 1984. Newfoundland Folklore Survey: Various Subjects. MUNFLA 84-340.

Renouf, E. 1971. MUNFLA FSC 71-27/25.

Rieti, B. 1991. *Strange Terrain: The Fairy World in Newfoundland.* Social and Economic Studies, No. 45. St. John's: Institute of Social and Economic Research.

Scheper-Hughes, N. 1979. *Saints, Scholars, and Schizophrenics.* Berkeley: University of California Press.

Sider, G. M. 1986. *Culture and Class in Anthropology and History: A Newfoundland Illustration.* New York: Cambridge University Press.

Southard, F. E. 1981. Aspects of Socio-economic Success in a Labrador Village. *Culture*, 1(1): 56–60.

———— 1982. Salt Cod and God: An Ethnography of Socio-economic Conditions Affecting Status in a Southern Labrador Community. M.A. thesis, Anthropology Department, Memorial University of Newfoundland, St. John's, Newfoundland.

Stopp, M. P., & K. Reynolds. 1992. *Preliminary Report of the 1992 Labrador South Coastal Survey.* Historic Resources Division, Department of Tourism and Culture. St. John's: M. P. Stopp Consulting.

Stopp, M. P. & D. Rutherford. 1991. *Preliminary Report of the 1991 South Labrador Coastal Archaeological Survey.* St. John's: M. P. Stopp Consulting.

Story, G. M., W. J. Kirwin, & J. D. A. Widdowson (eds.). 1982. *Dictionary of Newfoundland English.* Toronto: University of Toronto Press.

Strong, W. D. 1931. More Labrador Survivals. *American Speech* 6(4): 290–291.

Tanner, V. 1944. *Outlines of the Geography, Life and Customs of Newfoundland-Labrador.* Helsinki: Acta Geographica, 8.

Tachet, H., M. Lefebvre, & B. Thouron. 1758. Authorization, 20 March 1758, by Vaudrevil to creditors of Marsal to operate Cap Charles to expiration of concession in 1763. *PC* 7(1409): 3669.

Thompson, S. 1955–58. *Motif Index of Folk Literature*. Bloomington: Indiana University Press. (6 vols.).

Thornton, P. A. 1977. The Demographic and Mercantile Bases of Initial Permanent Settlement in the Strait of Belle Isle. In J. J. Mannion (ed.), *The Peopling of Newfoundland*. Social and Economic Papers, No. 8. St. John's: MUN Institute of Social and Economic Research.

Tönnies, F. [1887] 1957. *Gemeinschaft und Gesellschaft (Community and Society)*. East Lansing: Michigan State University Press.

Townsend, C. H. 1907. *Along the Labrador Coast*. Boston: Dana Estes.

Trudel, F. 1978. The Inuit of Southern Labrador and the Development of French Sedentary Fisheries (1700–1760). In R. J. Preston (ed.), *Canadian Ethnology Society, Papers from the Fourth Annual Congress, 1977*. National Museum of Man, Mercury Series, Canadian Ethnology Service, Paper No. 40. Ottawa: National Museums of Canada.

Tuck, J. A. 1982. Prehistoric Archaeology in Atlantic Canada Since 1975. *Canadian Journal of Archaeology* 6: 201–223.

———. 1975. *Prehistory of Saglek Bay, Labrador: Archaic and Palaeo-Eskimo Occupations*. Archaeological Survey of Canada, Paper No. 32. Ottawa: National Museums of Canada.

Vasina, J. 1985. *Oral Tradition as History*. Madison: University of Wisconsin Press.

Verge, J. 1967. MUNFLA FSC 67-21/125.

Von B. Neuhauser, D. 1959. Along the Way by Maraval. *ADSF* Oct.: 72–73.

Walsh, A. F. 1967. MUNFLA Q 67-1246.

Walsh, H. C. 1896. *The Last Cruise of the* Miranda: *A Record of Arctic Adventure*. New York: Transatlantic.

Widdowson, J. D. A. 1977. *If You Don't Be Good: Verbal Social Control in Newfoundland*. Newfoundland Social and Economic Studies No. 21. St. John's: Institute of Social and Economic Research.

Williams, H. J. 1979. Stories for Late at Night. *TD* 4(4): 4.

Wylie, J. 1982. The Sense of Time, the Social Construction of Reality, and the Foundations of Nationhood in Dominica and the Faroe Islands. *Comparative Studies in Society and History* 24(3): 438–466.